Government of India, Ministry of Railways

Railway Recruitment Board (RRB)

Centralized Employment Notification No. — RRC-01/2019

Group-D Level-I Exam – 2019

Assistant (Workshop), Assistant Bridge, Assistant C&W, Assistant Depot (Stores) Assistant Loco Shed (Diesel), Assistant Loco Shed (Electrical), Assistant Operations (Electrical), Assistant Pointsman, Assistant Signed & Telecom, Assistant Track Machine, Assistant TL&AC, Assistant TL&AC (Workshop), Assistant TRD, Assistant Work, Assistant Work (Workshop), Hospital Assistant and Track Maintainer Grade-IV

- General Knowledge
  - Current Affairs with Union Budget-2019-20
  - Indian Forest Survey Report-2017 (IFSR)
  - Indian Railways At a Glance
- General Science
  - Physics
  - Chemistry
  - Biology

Solved Papers RRB Group-D Exam-2017 & 2016

Edited & Compiled by

Diamond Power Learning Te...

DIAMOND POWER LEARNING

Production

Pushpendra

Published by

Diamond Power Learning

An imprint of

Diamond Pocket Books Pvt. Ltd.

X-30, Okhla Industrial Area, Phase–2, New Delhi-20

Tel : 91-011-40712200

e-mail : sales@dpb.in

Website : www.diamondbook.in

Contents

Railway Recruitement Board

Group-D Exam, 2017

1. **——— entered the Guinness World Records for recording the highest number of songs in several languages.**
(a) Shankar Mahadevan
(b) Sameer Anjaan
(c) P. Susheela
(d) Kavita Krishnamurthy

2. **Space research does NOT include the discipline ————.**
(a) Human culture
(b) Physics
(c) Biology
(d) Earth science

3. **A question and three statements labeled (I), (II) and (III) are given. You have to decide which statement(s) is/are sufficient to answer the question.**
Question :
How many people are in the queue?
Statements :
I. A man is 3rd from the beginning of the queue.
II. A man is 20th from the center of the queue.
III. A man is 7th from the end and 14th from the beginning.
Select the right option from the following.
(a) Only statement II is sufficient.
(b) Only statement I is sufficient.
(c) Data inadequate.
(d) Only statement III is sufficient.

4. **Chlorofluorocarbons are not used in ————**
(a) Refrigerators
(b) Mixer and grinders
(c) Air conditioners
(d) Packing materials

5. **Complete the analogy**
Illiterate : Educated : : Flood :
(a) Rain (b) Drought
(c) Well (d) River

6. **Archery is the national sport of which one of the following countries?**
(a) Turkey (b) China
(c) Bhutan (d) Japan

7. **Choose the best option and fill up the blank :**
'Ethnic' group of people, more appropriately, refers to people with a ————
(a) same behavior
(b) shared culture
(c) same genetic identity
(d) same nationality

8. **Which one of the following statements is incorrect?**
(a) Rational numbers do not include fractions.
(b) Real numbers which are not rational must be irrational.
(c) A real number is unique.
(d) Real numbers can be added, subtracted, multiplied or divided.

9. **MS Word is an example of :**
(a) Application Software
(b) Compiler
(c) Operating System
(d) System Software

10. **Arrange the numbers in descending order:**
$3\sqrt{5}, 2\sqrt{8}, 4\sqrt{6}$
(a) $4\sqrt{6} < 3\sqrt{5} < 2\sqrt{8}$
(b) $2\sqrt{8} > 4\sqrt{6} > 3\sqrt{5}$
(c) $4\sqrt{6} > 3\sqrt{5} > 2\sqrt{8}$
(d) $2\sqrt{8} > 3\sqrt{5} < 4\sqrt{6}$

11. X is the son of W and W is the brother of V. V is the sister of U. How is U related to X?

(a) Cannot be determined
(b) Daughter
(c) Mother
(d) Sister

12. St. Peter's Square is located in which of the following places?

(a) Athens (b) Berlin
(c) Washington (d) Vatican City

13. FDI stands for :

(a) Federal Department of Investment
(b) Forest Development Index
(c) Federal Department of Investigation
(d) Foreign Direct Investment

14. 17th Summit of the Non-Aligned Movement (NAM) was held in Venezuela with the slogan :

(a) United for Peace and Harmony
(b) United on the Path for Peace
(c) United on the Path of Global Peace
(d) United on the Path for Sustainable Peace

15. A statement followed by some conclusions are given below.

Statement : All drugs have side effects. So, there is always a built-in risk while taking medicines.

Conclusions :

I. No medicine is without the risk of side effects.

II. Drugs make things worse than the disease itself.

Find which of the given conclusions logically follows from the given statement.

(a) Only conclusion I follows
(b) Only conclusion II follows
(c) Neither I nor II follows
(d) Both I and II follow

16. Which one of the following has a terminating decimal expansion?

(a) $\frac{1}{6}$ (b) $\frac{17}{25}$
(c) $\frac{10}{3}$ (d) $\frac{1}{11}$

17. In science, which of the following is NOT the property of a mixture?

(a) The constituents of a mixture retain their properties.
(b) It is formed by two or more elements or compounds.
(c) It can be separated by physical methods.
(d) Its composition is fixed.

18. If LOGIC is written as IGCOL, then FRUIT is written as ———.

(a) TRFIU (b) RFTIU
(c) UTRFI (d) IUTRF

19. Replace the * signs in 25*5*35*20*2 with mathematical signs and find out which of the following options will give a balanced equation:

(a) $= \times \div +$ (b) $+ = \times \div$
(c) $\div + = \times$ (d) $\times \div + =$

20. ——— was the recipient of the Nobel Prize in Literature 2015.

(a) Paul Modrich
(b) Svetlana Alexievich
(c) William C. Campbell
(d) Takaaki Kajita

21. Simplify :

$1 \div [\{p^2 / (p+6)\} + \{6p / (p+6)\}]$

(a) $\frac{1}{p}$ (b) $\frac{1}{(p+6)}$
(c) $p + 6$ (d) p

22. $[(169 \times 121) \div (11 \times 13)] - 3 = ?$

(a) 135 (b) 140
(c) 137 (d) 143

23. If $\tan\theta = \frac{1}{\sqrt{5}}$, $\text{cosec}^2\theta = ?$

(a) 5 (b) $\sqrt{5}$
(c) $\sqrt{3}$ (d) 6

24. Gaurav Ghei is an Indian ———.

(a) Wrestler (b) Boxer
(c) Golfer (d) Badminton player

25. The Indian Railway Board Act was passed in the year :

(a) 1905 (b) 1890
(c) 1937 (d) 1966

26. **<u>Choose the most appropriate description</u> :**
National Bank for Agriculture and Rural Development is a ——.
(a) Self Help Group
(b) Commercial Bank
(c) Small and Medium Enterprise
(d) Supervisory Institution

27. **Lala Lajpat Rai hailed from—.**
(a) Uttar Pradesh
(b) Andhra Pradesh
(c) Punjab
(d) West Bengal

28. **Ben Kingsley is associated with——.**
(a) Pop Music
(b) Space travel
(c) Scientific research
(d) Motion pictures

29. **G and H can do a work in 30 days. If H alone can do it in 50 days, then G alone can do it in ———days.**
(a) 75 (b) 70
(c) 60 (d) 65

30. **Two varieties of rice, A and B, costing Rs. 210 and Rs. 280 per kg respectively are mixed in the ratio of 3 : 4. The mixed variety is sold at Rs. 260 per kg. What is the profit percentage?**
(a) 6% (b) 5%
(c) 32% (d) 4%

31. **B is the only son of C who has no daughter. K is the wife of the grandson of C. What is B to K?**
(a) Brother
(b) Father
(c) Father-in-law
(d) Son

32. **Akbar's seat of Government was ———.**
(a) Allahabad (b) Lucknow
(c) Delhi (d) Agra

33. **A circular ground of radius 7 m is surrounded by a path of width 3.5 m. Find the area of the path $\left(\pi = \frac{22}{7}\right)$**
(a) 202 sq.m (b) 154 sq.m
(c) 192.5 sq.m (d) 346.5 sq.m

34. **P, Q and R can do a work in 10, 15 and 30 days respectively. P works daily. Q and R together join p on alternate days starting the first day. In how many days will the work be done?**
(a) $6\frac{1}{3}$ (b) $6\frac{3}{4}$
(c) $6\frac{1}{2}$ (d) 6

35. **Find the missing letter (?) in the series :**
B, Z, W, S, N, ?
(a) J (b) G
(c) H (d) I

36. **What is the fourth proportional to 14, 6, 28 ?**
(a) 12 (b) 3
(c) 7 (d) 6

37. **Complete the analogy.**
CD : GA : : PQ : ?
(a) SM (b) SN
(c) US (d) TN

38. **——— species are NOT in the IUCN classification of threatened species.**
(a) Harmful (b) Extinct
(c) Vulnerable (d) Endangered

39. **The simple interest on a sum deposited at 8% pa. for 8 years is Rs. 16,000. What will be the compound interest on the same sum at one fourth of the above rate of interest for 2 years?**
(a) Rs. 1, 020 (b) Rs. 980
(c) Rs. 1,010 (d) Rs. 1,015

40. **Study the given statements and select the appropriate answer option based on them.**

Statements :

I. V is not shorter than A.

II. D is shorter than V.

III. A is shorter than D.

(a) D is shorter than A

(b) A is shorter than V and D

(c) A is taller than V.

(d) D is shorter than A and V

41. Which one of the following best describes the term 'capital gains tax' in the India?

(a) Tax on dividend received from corporate bonds.

(b) Tax on profit from sale of a capital asset during a year.

(c) Tax on interest received from bank fixed deposits.

(d) Tax on profit from sale of shares held for more than 12 months.

42. D can do a work in 18 days and E can do the same work in half that time. How many days will they take to finish the work, doing it together?

(a) 5 (b) 4

(c) 7 (d) 6

43. 15 laptops were purchased at Rs. 15,000 each and all of them were sold for Rs. 2.97 Lakh. Find the profit percentage.

(a) 28% (b) 40%

(c) 33.33% (d) 32%

44. In which year, did Mahatma Gandhi return to India from South Africa?

(a) 1905 (b) 1920

(c) 1915 (d) 1910

45. An amount is deposited at 8% p.a. compound interest. If the first year interest is Rs.72, find the interest amount for the 2nd year.

(a) 77.56 (b) 77.64

(c) 77.76 (d) 85.77

46. Complete the analogy.
Grief : Happiness : : Diffidence :

(a) Ignorance (b) Sorrow

(c) Confidence (d) Cowardice

47. N has Rs. p more than K. The total amount available with N and K together is Rs. q. How much does K have?

(a) $\frac{q}{2}+p$ (b) 2 (p + q)

(c) $\frac{(p+q}{2}$ (d) $\frac{(q-p)}{2}$

48. Find the value of 'x' in $x : \frac{3}{7} :: \frac{7}{9} : \frac{5}{9}$

(a) $\frac{4}{7}$ (b) $\frac{3}{2}$

(c) $\frac{3}{5}$ (d) $\frac{9}{7}$

49. Find the mode of the following data : 70, 80, 65, 90, 70, 90, 80, 70, 75, 65

(a) 90 (b) 80

(c) 70 (d) 65

50. Find the missing term (?) in the alphabetical series :
AC, DG, HL, ? SY, ...

(a) NQ (b) NR

(c) MQ (d) MR

51. (1 + 2/3) ÷ [(1 + 1/3) ÷ (2/3 +1)] = ?

(a) $\frac{4}{3}$ (b) $\frac{3}{4}$

(c) $\frac{12}{25}$ (d) $\frac{25}{12}$

52. Which one of the following is NOT an Omnivore?

(a) Rat (b) Ant

(c) Bear (d) Snake

53. If P : Q : R is 1/3 : 2/3 : 1/4 and Q = 56, then P –R = ?

(a) 5 (b) 8

(c) 6 (d) 7

54. 'Mission Raftaar' project is associated with :

(a) Air transport

(b) Road transport

(c) Water transport

(d) Rail transport

55. ——— cannot be corrected with spectacles.

(a) Presbyopia (b) Hypermetropia

(c) Cataract (d) Myopia

Directions (56-59)

Comprehension :

In a district, there are four electoral constituencies. Four political parties put up their candidates. The number of votes polled by each party, in thousands, is given below.

Constituency	Party I	Party II	Party III	Party IV
East	180	74	56	34
South	8	70	108	210
North	72	275	44	225
West	19	23	101	191

56. By how many more votes, did party IV win the South constituency than the next highest party?

(a) 0.7 Lakh (b) 1.02 Lakh
(c) 1. 08 Lakh (d) 2.10 Lakh

57. Which party won more than one constituency in the district?

(a) Party I (b) Party III
(c) Party II (d) Party IV

58. Which constituency has the highest total number of votes polled?

(a) West (b) North
(c) East (d) South

59. Which party polled the highest number of votes in the district as whole?

(a) Party II (b) Party I
(c) Party III (d) Party IV

Directions (60-62)

Comprehension :

P, Q, R, S, T and U follow different professions. There is a politician, an actor, a banker, an ex-serviceman, a nurse and a housewife. Consider the following information and answer the questions based on it.

(a) R is the ex-serviceman married to a housewife.
(b) Q is an actor whose brother T is not a politician.
(c) U is neither a banker nor a politician.
(d) P is the wife of R

60. Who is the banker?

(a) R (b) T
(c) Q (d) P

61. Who is the politician?

(a) S (b) U
(c) T (d) R

62. Who is the nurse?

(a) P (b) T
(c) U (d) S

63. The first pair of words has a certain relation. Find the word with the same relation to complete the next pair.

River : Bank : : Sea : ?

(a) Shore (b) Creek
(c) Bay (d) Sand

64. Which one of the following is NOT a children welfare scheme?

(a) Inclusive education for the disabled at secondary stage
(b) Sarva Shikha Abhiyan
(c) Swayamsiddha
(d) Right to Education

65. A man buy a refrigerator Rs. 22,000 and pays an additional Rs. 1,000 for transport and Rs. 2,000 for installation. What should be the selling price to get a profit of 15% on the whole transaction?

(a) Rs. 27,250 (b) Rs. 28,500
(c) Rs. 28,750 (d) Rs. 29,250

66. What do we call those who study the Earth and its land, features and inhabitants, as?

(a) Historians
(b) Farmers
(c) Geographers
(d) Biographers

67. Find the HCF of 143, 77 and 121.

(a) 6 (b) 11
(c) 4 (d) 7

68. Find the incorrect number in the series:

6, 11, 16, 20, 26 ......

(a) 20 (b) 6
(c) 26 (d) 16

69. Which one of the following is not an energy converter?

(a) Solar panel (b) Steam engine
(c) Plain glass (d) Electric iron

70. Find the LCM of 24, 96 and 36.

(a) 576 (b) 216
(c) 288 (d) 144

71. CD-ROM is a ________

(a) MP3 file
(b) Microprocessor
(c) Magnetic disk
(d) Storage medium

72. A lady said, "Sonia is the daughter of the only daughter of my father." How is the lady related to Sonia?

(a) Mother (b) Daughter
(c) Sister (d) Grandmother

73. ________ was NOT declared a World Heritage site by UNESCO.

(a) Matheran Hill Railway
(b) Darjeeling Himalayan Railways
(c) Kalka Shimla Railway line
(d) Nilgiri Mountain Rail

74. If a political party is treated as a recognised political party in _____ or more states, it shall be known as a 'National Party' throughout the whole of India.

(a) 4 (b) 2
(c) 3 (d) 1

75. An assertion (A) and a reason (R) are given below.

Assertion (A): Nowadays, more people opt for fast food.

Reason (R): Fast food is always inexpensive.

Choose the correct option.

(a) Both A and R are true, but R is not the correct explanation of A
(b) A is false, but R is true
(c) A is true, but R is false
(d) Both A and R are true and R is the correct explanation of A

76. Who was selected as the captain for the Men's ICC World T20 XI 2016?

(a) M S Dhoni
(b) Darren Sammy
(c) Shane Watson
(d) Virat Kohli

77. Complete the analogy.
If ADC = 12, BEC = ?

(a) 30 (b) 28
(c) 24 (d) 18

78. Rearrange the jumbled letter to make a meaningful English word and then select the word which is different from the rest.

(a) AFMR (b) NDAL
(c) PLCA (d) TLPNA

79. The simple interest at R% p.a. on a certain principal P is $\left(\frac{9}{16}\right)^{th}$ of P. If R is equal to the number of years (N), find the value of N.

(a) 8.5 (b) 7
(c) 7.5 (d) 6

80. What is 40% of $\frac{3}{5}$ th of 24?

(a) 14.4 (b) 5.76
(c) 7.2 (d) 9.6

81. The World Heritage Site having the architectural work of Le Corbusier is located in:

(a) Kochi (b) Chandigarh
(c) Goa (d) Puducherry

82. Which one of the following states does NOT have the Indian Elephant as its State animal?

(a) Assam (b) Karnataka
(c) Kerala (d) Jharkhand

83. A statement followed by some conclusions are given below.

Statement : Nowadays, life has become very difficult without a mobile phone.

Conclusions :

I. Total number of mobile subscribers is increasing.

II. Mobile has become an integral part of life.

Find which of the given conclusions logically follows from the given statement.

(a) Only conclusion I follows
(b) Neither I nor II follows
(c) Both I and II follows
(d) Only conclusion II follows

84. A question and three statements labeled (I), (II) and (III) are given. You have to decide which statement(s) is/are sufficient to answer the question.

Question : Find the present age of Y.

Statements :

I. At present, X is 3 times as old as Y.

II. X and Y started schooling in the same year.

III. After 5 years, the age of X will be 2 1/2 times that of Y.

Select the right option from the following.

(a) Both statements I and II are sufficient.
(b) Both statements II and III are sufficient
(c) Only statement I is sufficient.
(d) Both statements I and III are sufficient.

85. The first pair of words has a certain relation.

Find the word with the same relation to complete the next pair.

Jupiter : Europa : : Earth : ?

(a) Apollo (b) Sun
(c) Phobos (d) Moon

86. Car I covers a distance in a certain time. Car II takes double the time to cover half the same distance. Find the ratio of their respective speeds.

(a) 1 : 2 (b) 1 : 4
(c) 2 : 1 (d) 4 : 1

87. Complete the analogy.

B : 8 : : C : ?

(a) 27 (b) 10
(c) 24 (d) 11

88. Which of the following is NOT an environmental Problem?

(a) Genetic modification of food
(b) Afforestation
(c) Acid Rain
(d) Loss of Biodiversity

89. Speeds greater than the speed of sound in air are known as _______.

(a) Supersonic (b) Solar
(c) Infrasonic (d) Ultrasonic

90. What is the next term in the following alphabetical series?

ACBD, FHGI, KMLN, ?

(a) OQPR (b) PRQS
(c) PQRS (d) OPQR

91. Which one is NOT true with electromagnets?

(a) It is a temporary magnet.
(b) Its strength varies with the air gap between its poles.
(c) Polarity cannot be changed.
(d) Its strength can be changed

92. Plants and micro-organisms help in recreating the quality of ______.

(a) our lifestyle
(b) our wealth
(c) outer space
(d) the air we breathe

93. The areas of two similar triangles are 169 sq.cm and 121 sq.cm. If the longest side of larger triangle is 26 cm, then the length of the longest side of the other triangle is ______.

(a) 26 cm (b) 18 cm
(c) 28 cm (d) 22 cm

94. If a student's marks were increased by 25% he would have scored 75 in his test. How much did he actually score?

(a) 60 (b) 50
(c) 15 (d) 25

95. A formula in MS Excel starts with a _____ symbol.

(a) + (b) =

(c) # (d) @

96. If the mean of distribution 10, 8, 15, 12, K, 25 is 12, find the value of K.

(a) 2 (b) 1

(c) 4 (d) 3

97. Find the missing number (?) in the following series.

1, 1.5, 2.5, 4, ?, 8.5, 11.5, ...

(a) 6 (b) 5

(c) 4.5 (d) 5.5

98. Which of the following is a non-food crop?

(a) Fiber crops (b) Coffee

(c) Oil seeds (d) Sugarcane

99. Find the least square number which is exactly divisible by 4, 9 and 14.

(a) 1008 (b) 252

(c) 1764 (d) 504

100. One of the conditions for recognition of a political party as a State party as a in India is that it secures at least ______ % of the valid votes polled at the last general election in the State to the Legislative Assembly.

(a) 4 (b) 5

(c) 3 (d) 6

Answer Sheet

1. (c)	**2.** (a)	**3.** (d)	**4.** (b)	**5.** (b)	**6.** (c)	**7.** (b)	**8.** (a)	**9.** (a)	**10.** (a)
11. (a)	**12.** (d)	**13.** (d)	**14.** (b)	**15.** (a)	**16.** (b)	**17.** (d)	**18.** (d)	**19.** (c)	**20.** (b)
21. (a)	**22.** (b)	**23.** (d)	**24.** (c)	**25.** (a)	**26.** (d)	**27.** (c)	**28.** (d)	**29.** (a)	**30.** (d)
31. (c)	**32.** (d)	**33.** (c)	**34.** (c)	**35.** (c)	**36.** (a)	**37.** (d)	**38.** (a)	**39.** (c)	**40.** (b)
41. (b)	**42.** (d)	**43.** (d)	**44.** (c)	**45.** (c)	**46.** (c)	**47.** (d)	**48.** (c)	**49.** (c)	**50.** (c)
51. (d)	**52.** (d)	**53.** (d)	**54.** (d)	**55.** (c)	**56.** (b)	**57.** (d)	**58.** (b)	**59.** (d)	**60.** (b)
61. (a)	**62.** (c)	**63.** (a)	**64.** (c)	**65.** (c)	**66.** (c)	**67.** (b)	**68.** (a)	**69.** (c)	**70.** (c)
71. (d)	**72.** (a)	**73.** (a)	**74.** (a)	**75.** (c)	**76.** (d)	**77.** (a)	**78.** (c)	**79.** (c)	**80.** (b)
81. (b)	**82.** (a)	**83.** (d)	**84.** (d)	**85.** (d)	**86.** (d)	**87.** (a)	**88.** (b)	**89.** (a)	**90.** (b)
91. (c)	**92.** (d)	**93.** (d)	**94.** (a)	**95.** (b)	**96.** (a)	**97.** (a)	**98.** (a)	**99.** (c)	**100.** (d)

Explanations

10. (a) $2\sqrt{8} = 4\sqrt{2}$

$\therefore (3\sqrt{5})^2 = 9 \times 5 = 45$

$\left(4\sqrt{2}\right)^2 = 16 \times 2 = 32$

$\left(4\sqrt{6}\right)^2 = 16 \times 6 = 96$

$\therefore 4\sqrt{6} > 3\sqrt{5} > 4\sqrt{2}$

11. (a) X is the son of W/X
W is the brother of U and V/W
V is the sister of U and W/V
U is uncle or aunt of X/U

15. (a) All drugs (Without any exception) have side effects. Therefore, there is no medicine without the risk of side effects. Thus, only Conclusion I follows.

19. (c) 25 ∗5 ∗35∗ 20∗ 2
$\Rightarrow 25 \div 5 + 35 = 20 \times 2$
$\Rightarrow 5 + 35 = 20 \times 2$
$\Rightarrow 40 = 40$

21. (a) $1 \div \left(\frac{p^2}{p+6} + \frac{6p}{p+6}\right)$

$= 1 \div \left(\frac{p^2 + 6p}{p+6}\right)$

$= 1 \div \left(\frac{p\,(p+6)}{p+6}\right)$

$= 1 \div p = \frac{1}{p}$

22. (b) $? = \frac{169 \times 121}{11 \times 13} - 3$

$= 11 \times 13 - 3 = 143 - 3 = 140$

23. (d) $\tan\theta = \frac{1}{\sqrt{5}}$

$\Rightarrow \cot\theta = \sqrt{5}$

$\therefore \text{cosec}^2\theta = 1 + \cot^2\theta$

$= 1 + \left(\sqrt{5}\right)^2 = 1 + 5 = 6$

29. (a) (G + H)' s 1 day's work (G +H) = $\frac{1}{30}$

H's 1 day's work = $\frac{1}{50}$

$\therefore$ G's 1 day's work

$= \frac{1}{30} - \frac{1}{50} = \frac{5-3}{150} = \frac{1}{75}$

$\therefore$ Required time = 75 days

30. (d) C.P. of 7 kg. of mixture.
= Rs (3 × 210 + 4 × 280)
= Rs 630 × 11200 = Rs. 1750
Total S.P. = Rs. (7 × 260)
= Rs 1820
Profit = Rs. 1820 – 1750
= Rs 70
$\therefore$ Profit per cent

$= \frac{70}{1750} \times 100 = 4\%$

31. (c) C has no daughter
B is the only son of C
K is the wife of the grandson of C
It means K is the wife of B's son.
Therefore, B is the father-in-law of K.

33. (c)

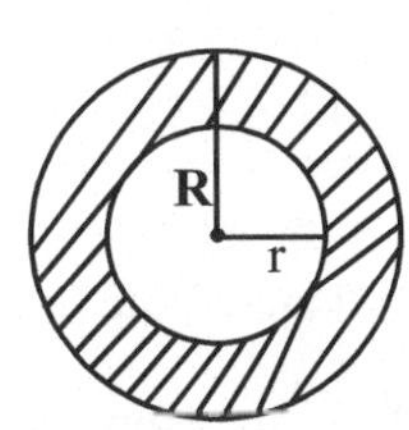

R = (7 + 3.50) metre
= 10.5 metre

r = 7 metre

∴ Area of the path

$= \pi (R^2 - r^2) = \pi (R + r) (R - r)$

$= \frac{22}{7} (10.5 + 7) (10.5 - 7)$

$= \frac{22}{7} \times 17.5 \times 3.5$

= 192.5 square cm

34. (c) According to the question

Work done in first 2 days

= (P + Q + R)'s 1 day's work + P's 1 day's work

$= \frac{1}{10} + \frac{1}{15} + \frac{1}{30} + \frac{1}{10}$

$= \frac{2}{10} + \frac{1}{15} + \frac{1}{30}$

$= \frac{6+2+1}{30} = \frac{9}{30} = \frac{3}{10}$

∴ Work done in first 6 days $= \frac{9}{10}$

Remaining work $= \frac{1}{10}$ which will be done by all

three (P + Q + R) in $\frac{1}{2}$ day.

∴ Total time $= 6\frac{1}{2}$ days

36. (a) According to the question

$\frac{14}{6} = \frac{28}{x}$

$\Rightarrow 14x = 28 \times 6$

$\Rightarrow x = \frac{28 \times 6}{14} = 12$

39. (c) Principal $= \frac{\text{S.I} \times 100}{\text{Time} \times \text{Rate}}$

$= \frac{1600 \times 100}{8 \times 8} = \text{Rs } 2500$

Case II, Rate = 2% per annum

$\therefore \text{C.I.} = P\left[\left(1 + \frac{R}{100}\right)^T - 1\right]$

$= 25000 \left[\left(1 + \frac{2}{100}\right)^2 - 1\right]$

$= 25000 [(1.02)^2 - 1]$

= 25000 (1.0404 – 1)

25000 × 0.0404 = Rs. 1010

42. (d) Time taken by D = 18 days

∴ Time taken by E = 9 days

∴ (D + E)'s 1 days work

$= \frac{1}{18} + \frac{1}{9} = \frac{1+2}{18} = \frac{1}{6}$

∴ Required time = 6 days

43. (d) Total C.P. of 15 laptops

= Rs. (15 × 15000)

= Rs. 225000

Total S. P. = Rs. 297000

Profit = Rs. (297000–225000)

= Rs.72000

∴ Profit percent

$= \frac{72000}{225000} \times 100 = 32\%$

45. (c) Let the principal be Rs. P.

∴ 8% of P = 72

$\Rightarrow \frac{P \times 8}{100} = 72$

$\Rightarrow P = \frac{72 \times 100}{8} = \text{Rs.}900$

For second year

Principal Rs. (900 +72) = Rs.972

∴ Required interest = 8% of Rs. 972

$= \text{Rs.} \left(\frac{972 \times 8}{100}\right) = \text{Rs.}77.76$

47. (d) N = k + p

N + k = q

$\Rightarrow k + p + k = q$

$\Rightarrow 2k = q - p$

$\Rightarrow k = \frac{q - p}{2}$

48. (c) $x : \frac{3}{7} = \frac{7}{9} : \frac{5}{9}$

$\Rightarrow x \times \frac{5}{9} = \frac{3}{7} \times \frac{7}{9} = \frac{1}{3}$

$\Rightarrow x = \frac{1}{3} \times \frac{9}{5} = \frac{3}{5}$

50. (d)

$A \xrightarrow{+3} D \xrightarrow{+4} H \xrightarrow{+5} \boxed{M} \xrightarrow{+6} S$

$C \xrightarrow{+4} G \xrightarrow{+5} L \xrightarrow{+6} \boxed{R} \xrightarrow{+7} Y$

53. (d) $P : Q : R = \frac{1}{3} : \frac{2}{3} : \frac{1}{4}$

$= \frac{1}{3} \times 12 : \frac{2}{3} \times 12 : \frac{1}{4} \times 12$

$= 4 : 8 : 3$

$Q = 8k = 56$

$\Rightarrow k = 56 \div 8 = 7 = P–R$

56. (b) Required difference
$= (210 - 108) \times 1000$
$= 102000 = 1.02$ lakh

57. (d) Party IV won south and west constituencies.

58. (b) Total votes polled in north constituency = (72 + 275 + 44 + 225) thousand = 616 thousand

59. (d) Total votes got by party IV
(34 + 210 + 225 + 191) thousand = 660

65. (c) Actual cost price of refrigerator

= Rs. (22000 + 1000 + 2000)

= Rs. 25000

For a gain of 15%,

Its S.P = Rs. $\left(\frac{25000 \times 115}{100}\right)$

= Rs. 28750

67. (b) $143 = 11 \times 13$

$77 = 11 \times 7$

$121 = 11 \times 11$

$\therefore$ Required HCF = 11

70. (c) $24 = 2 \times 12$

$96 = 8 \times 12 = 2^3 \times 12$

$36 = 3 \times 12$

$\therefore$ Required LCM

$= 12 \times 3 \times 8 = 288$

77. (a)

A ↓ 1, D ↓ 4, C ↓ 3

$1 \times 4 \times 3 = 12$

Therefore,

B ↓ 2, E ↓ 5, C ↓ 3

$2 \times 5 \times 3 = 30$

79. (c) $\frac{\text{Interest}}{\text{Principal}} = \frac{9}{16}$

$\therefore \text{Rate} = \frac{\text{Interest}}{\text{Principal}} \times \frac{100}{\text{Time}}$

$\Rightarrow N = \frac{9}{16} \times \frac{100}{N}$

$\Rightarrow N^2 = \frac{900}{16}$

$\Rightarrow N = \sqrt{\frac{900}{16}} = \frac{30}{4} = 7.5$

80. **(b)** $? = 24 \times \frac{3}{5} \times \frac{40}{100} = 5.76$

86. (d) Required ratio = $\frac{s}{t} : \frac{\frac{s}{2}}{2t}$

$= \frac{s}{t} : \frac{s}{4t} = 4 : 1$

87. **(a)** B $\Rightarrow$ 2, i.e, Position number in the English alphabetical series.

Now : $2 \times 2 \times 2 = 3$

Therefore : C $\Rightarrow$ 3

And $3 \times 3 \times 3 = 27$

93. (d)

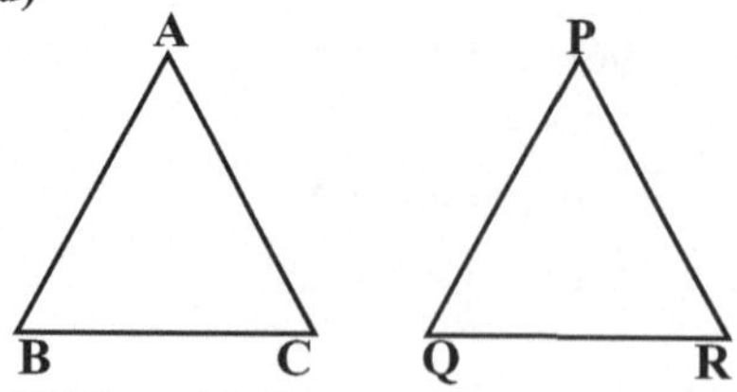

$\Delta ABC \sim \Delta PQR$

$$\therefore \frac{\text{Area of } \Delta ABC}{\text{Area of } \Delta PQR} = \frac{AB^2}{PQ^2}$$

$$\frac{\Delta ABC \text{ का क्षेत्रफल}}{\Delta AQR \text{ का क्षेत्रफल}} = \frac{AB^2}{PQ^2}$$

$$\Rightarrow \frac{169}{121} = \frac{AB^2}{PQ^2}$$

$$\Rightarrow \frac{13}{11} = \frac{AB}{PQ}$$

$$\Rightarrow \frac{13}{11} = \frac{26}{PQ}$$

$$\Rightarrow PQ = \frac{26 \times 11}{13} = 22\text{cm}$$

94. (a) Let original marks of the student be ***x***.
According to the question

$$x \times \frac{125}{100} = 75$$

$$\Rightarrow x = \frac{75 \times 100}{125} = 60$$

99. (c) LCM of 4, 9 and 14

$4 = 2 \times 2$

$9 = 3 \times 3$

$14 = 2 \times 7$

$\therefore$ LCM $= 2 \times 2 \times 3 \times 3 \times 7$

$= 2^2 \times 3^2 \times 7$

$\therefore$ Required number

$= 2^2 \times 3^2 \times 7^2 = 1764$

Railway Recruitement Board

Group-D Exam, 2016

Directions (1-3):

Answer the question on the following table: Assume all colleges sent equal number of candidates in all subjects for the Examination

Percentage of passed students by subject

College	Maths	Physics	Chemistry	Botany	Zoology
P	52	65	62	40	47
Q	47	62	52	38	35
R	53	70	46	39	54
S	35	72	58	57	62

1. **Seeing the performance of all the four colleges together which combination of groups has shown the lowest level of passed students?**
   (a) Chemistry and Botany
   (b) Physics and Chemistry
   (c) Zoology and Botany
   (d) Mathematics and Physics
2. **Taking the perfomance in all the subjects into account, which college has shown the higest level of passed students?**
   (a) P (b) S
   (c) R (d) Q
3. **Taking all the college into account which subject has shown the lowest number of passed students?**
   (a) Chemistry (b) Botany
   (c) Physics (d) Mathematics
4. **If '+' means '×', '×' means '–', '–' means '÷' and '÷' means '+' then $32 \div 8 - 2 \times 12 + 4 =$**
   (a) 12 (b) –12
   (c) 21 (d) 13
5. **Study of atmosphere is called?**
   (a) Atmosphology
   (b) Meteorology
   (c) Ecology
   (d) Motellology
6. **Which of the following is an example for marsupials?**
   (a) Kangaroo (b) Whale
   (c) Giraffe (d) Rooster
7. **Who is the current President of ICC?**
   (a) Zaheer Abbas
   (b) Sharad Pawar
   (c) Ravi Shastri
   (d) Shashank Manohar
8. **Who is the Bollywood lyricist who created Guinness record for composing maximum number of songs?**
   (a) Anand Bakshi
   (b) Gulzar
   (c) Sahir Ludhianvi
   (d) Sameer Anjaan
9. **What does MMU stand for?**
   (a) Machine Memory Unit
   (b) Memory Management Unit
   (c) Main Memory Unit
   (d) Machine Management Unit
10. **Choose the odd one out**
    (a) Incisors (b) Canines
    (c) Molars (d) Bones
11. **Who was the first king of the Vijayanagara empire?**
    (a) Bukkaraya I
    (b) Krishnadevaraya
    (c) Harihara I
    (d) Ramadevaraya
12. **Where can you find Notre-Dame cathedral?**
    (a) California (b) Leeds
    (c) Belgium (d) Paris

13. During what period was P.A.Sangma, who died recently, the Lok Sabha Speaker?

(a) 1994-1996 (b) 1996-1998
(c) 1998-2002 (d) 2002-2004

14. The atomic number is represented by ——— in the nucleus.

(a) Protons (b) Neutrons
(c) Electrons (d) Hydrons

15. Where can we find the tallest statue of Jesus Christ in the World?

(a) Barzil (b) Mexico
(c) Italy (d) Peru

16. Which of the following means re-establishment of forest cover either naturally or artificially?

(a) Deforestation
(b) Afforestation
(c) Reforestation
(d) Hiforestation

17. Given a = 128, b = 130 and c = 132, Find the value of $a^3 + b^3 + c^3 - 3abc$.

(a) 5000 (b) 4680
(c) 4280 (d) 4890

18. Who is the 23rd governor of RBI?

(a) Bimal Jalan
(b) Raghuram Rajan
(c) D. Subba Rao
(d) Dr. Manmohan Singh

19. In certain code, PARIS is written as KZIRH. How is LONDON written in that code?

(a) OMLWLM (b) OLMWLM
(c) OLMLWM (d) OMWLWM

20. If the angles of a triangle are in the ratio of 1 : 4 : 7, then find the ratio of greatest and smallest angles to the smallest angle.

(a) 8 : 1 (b) 2 : 3
(c) 7 : 1 (d) 3 : 5

21. The mean of a distribution is 18 and the standard deviation is 7. What is the value of the coefficient variation?

(a) 50% (b) 76.77%
(c) 54.44% (d) 38.88%

22. Select the combination of numbers so that the letters arranged accordingly a form will meaningful word:

N	P	O	A	C	L	M	I
1	2	3	4	5	6	7	8

(a) 5, 3, 2, 7, 6, 4, 8, 1
(b) 5, 3, 7, 2, 6, 4, 8, 1
(c) 4, 7, 5, 1, 6, 8, 2, 3
(d) 1, 7, 8, 6, 4, 3, 2, 5,

23. Which planet is called the morning/ evening star?

(a) Mercury (b) Venus
(c) Mars (d) Saturn

24. A fraud shopkeeper sell his product at 100, instead of 85 and claims to sell at cost price. What is his profit percentage?

(a) 17.64% (b) 16.59%
(c) 13.65% (d) 15.64%

25. What is the SI unit of force?

(a) Kelvin (b) Newton
(c) Pascal (d) Volt

26. Based on the analogy given, find the missing number from the given options.

0.16: 0.0016 : : 1.02 : ———

(a) 0.0102 (b) 10.02
(c) 0.012 (d) 1.0102

27. A metro train of length 125 m crosses a metro station of length 75m in 10 seconds. What is the speed of metro train?

(a) 72 km/hr (b) 36 km/hr
(c) 18 km/hr (d) 90 km/hr

28. If cosA = 12/13, then Sin A (1- tan A) = ?

(a) 32/135 (b) 32/137
(c) 35/152 (d) 35/156

29. Consider the following statements & choose the correct options:

When two straight lines intersect then,

(1) Adjacent angles are complementary
(2) Opposite angles are equal
(a) Both 1 & 2 are incorrect
(b) Both 1 & 2 are correct
(c) 1 is incorrect and 2 is correct
(d) 1 is correct and 2 is incorrect

30. What is a machine-readable code in the form of numbers and a pattern of parallel lines of varying widths called?
(a) Morse codes
(b) Passcodes
(c) Bar codes
(d) Pin codes

31. A is 3 time more efficient than B, ratio of number of days taken to complete a work X by A and B are in the ratio of
(a) 1 : 3 (b) 4 : 1
(c) 1 : 4 (d) 3 : 1

32. Which of the following rivers has its origin in Tibet?
(a) Godavari
(b) Mahanadi
(c) Brahmaputra
(d) Son

33. Who was called the Frontier Gandhi?
(a) Mahatma Gandhi
(b) Khan Abdul Ghaffar Khan
(c) C.Rajagopalachari
(d) Lala Lajpat Rai

34. Find the HCF of 0.32, 2.72, 12.8, 14.4
(a) 16 (b) 1.6
(c) 0.16 (d) 2.72

35. How many pairs of eyes do spiders have?
(a) 1 (b) 2
(c) 4 (d) 8

36. An Assertion (A) and a Reason (R) are given below.
Assertion (A): A little gap is left between iron rails.
Reason (R): Iron expands in summer.
Choose the correct option.
(a) A is true but R is false.
(b) A is false but R is true.
(c) Both A and R are true and R is the correct explanation of A.
(d) Both A and R are true but R is not the correct explanation of A.

37. If $2^x - 2^{x-1} = 8$, then find the value of $2x^2 + 4x + 3$
(a) 41 (b) 20
(c) 21 (d) 51

38. What is a celestial object consisting of a nucleus of ice and dust called?
(a) Star (b) Moon
(c) Comet (d) Asteroid

39. The mean of 8 observations is 10. Three mole observations are included and the new mean becomes 12. The mean of the three new observations is
(a) 16 (b) 18
(c) 17.33 (d) 15

40. In what time will Rs. 10, 000 deposited in a bank will amount to Rs. 13, 310 at 10% per annum compounded annually?
(a) 4 years (b) 5 years
(c) 3 years (d) 6 years

41. If the cloud is called blue, blue is called rain, rain is called black, black is called air, air is called yellow and yellow is called water, where will the birds fly?
(a) Blue (b) Air
(c) Yellow (d) Black

42. By using formula of mean proportional and third proportional, find the ratio of third proportional to 8 and 20 and mean proportional between 4 and 9.
(a) 21 : 6 (b) 25 : 3
(c) 24 : 5 (d) 5 : 2

43. Which of the following is an input device?
(a) Monitor (b) Printer
(c) Floppy disk (d) Joy stick

44. Which Pallava King also wrote Sanskrit plays?
(a) Raja Raja Chola
(b) Mahendravarman I
(c) Rajasimha
(d) Vikramaditya

45. From an aeroplane vertically above a straight road the angle of depression of two stones on the same side are 30° and 45°. What is the distance between two stones if the aeroplane is flying at a height of 1.365 km?
(a) 1 km (b) 2 km
(c) 3 km (d) 4 km

46. If (4y + 55)° and (3y + 69)° are supplementary angles then find value of y.
(a) 10 (b) 6
(c) 12 (d) 8

47. When was the formal proclamation to Swadeshi movement made?
(a) December 15, 1905
(b) August 7, 1905
(c) February 26, 1906
(d) July 18, 1905

48. The enrichment of an ecosystem with chemical nutrients, typically compounds containing nitrogen, phosphorus is called
(a) Eutrophication
(b) Sedimentation
(c) Hydrogenation
(d) Oxidation

49. Cache memory is a
(a) RAM (b) ROM
(c) EROM (d) EPROM

50. Below are given statements followed by two conclusions I and II. You have to take the given statements to be true even if they seem to be at variance from commonly known facts.

Statements: Some papers are pencils.
Some pencils are erasers.
All erasers are boxes.

Conclusions: **I.** Some erasers are papers.
II. Some papers are boxes.

Decide which of the below options logically follows the given Statement.
(a) Only conclusion I follows
(b) Only conclusion II follows
(c) Both conclusion I and II follow
(d) Neither conclusion I nor II follow

51. If the standard deviation of a population is 6, what would be the population variance?
(a) 6 (b) 12
(c) 24 (d) 36

52. If $3x^2 + 4y^2 - 8xy - 2x + 1 = 0$, then find the value of $(x + y)^2$
(a) 3 (b) 4
(c) 5 (d) 6

53. Find the difference between the largest and smallest fraction :

3/5, 5/9, 7/9, 2/5

(a) 9/17 (b) 6/7
(c) 17/45 (d) 13/17

54. At certain rate of simple interest, Rs. 800 amounts to Rs. 956 in 3 years. If this sum amounts to Rs. 1052 in same period, find increase in rate percentage.
(a) 7% (b) 4%
(c) 5% (d) 9.5%

55. Find total prime factor in the product of $\{(16)^7 \times (27)^6 \times 5^9\}$
(a) 28 (b) 43
(c) 55 (d) 56

56. Presence of what in high level of the following leads to diabates?
(a) Fructose (b) Sucrose
(c) Glucose (d) Saccharides

57. Which Chief Minister has held office as the longest serving Chief Minister till date?
(a) Joyti Basu
(b) Pawan Kumar Chamling
(c) M.G. Ramachandran
(d) E. K. Nayanar

Direction (58-60): Study the following information carefully and answer the questions given below it.

Ajith is the son of Kumar. Susmitha, Kumar's sister, has a son Deepak and a daughter Harishma. Babu is the maternal uncle of Deepak.

58. How is Ajith related to Deepak?

(a) Nephew (b) Brother
(c) Uncle (d) Cousin

59. How many nephews does Babu have?

(a) One (b) Two
(c) Three (d) Nil

60. How is Harishma related to Babu?

(a) Daughter (b) Niece
(c) Sister (d) Wife

61. Which day is observed as the Constitution day in India?

(a) 26th November
(b) 15th August
(c) 14th April
(d) 6th December

62. Who invented the revolver?

(a) William Hunt
(b) Robert H. Goddard
(c) Henry Ogle
(d) Samuel Colt

63. If W > X, X > Y AND Y > Z, then which of the following conclusions is definitely wrong?

(a) Z > W (b) W > Z
(c) W > Y (d) X > Z

64. According to ICC test rankings, which player is ranked first?

(a) Virat Kohli
(b) AB de villiers
(c) Steve Smith
(d) Aaron Finch

65. In a college, 30 students can build 60% of a project in 5 days, what % of project can be built by 45 students in 2 days?

(a) 36% (b) 45%
(c) 33% (d) 32%

66. MRP on the pack of any product refers to

(a) Marginal Retail Price
(b) Maximum Retail Price
(c) Monopoly Retail Product
(d) Maximum Recycled Product

67. Based on the analogy given, find the missing pair from the given options.

11 : 1210 : : ——— : ———

(a) 9 : 729 (b) 8 : 448
(c) 6 : 216 (d) 7 : 1029

68. What is the maximum score that can be scored in a game of ten-pin bowling?

(a) 100 (b) 200
(c) 300 (d) 400

69. Which among the following is a prosthetic leg?

(a) Athletes foot
(b) Jaipur foot
(c) Crowfoot
(d) Tender foot

70. Anusha bought a sandal at $7/10^{th}$ of its selling price and sold it at 10% more than its selling price. Find her gain percent.

(a) 55.54% (b) 57.14%
(c) 53.14% (d) 52.24%

71. Where will you be if you were on Filitheyo island?

(a) Sri Lanka
(b) Lakshadweep
(c) Maldives
(d) Thailand

72. Choose the one which is different or odd from the following options.

(a) NEXFL (b) ZGPKU
(c) LANCP (d) FRGSP

73. If ‘<’ denotes ‘–’, ‘+’denotes ‘÷’, ‘>’denotes ‘+’, ‘–’ denotes ‘=’ ‘=’ denotes ‘<’ and ‘×’ denotes‘ >’, then which of the following statement is true?

(a) $3 > 2 < 4 \times 8 + 4 < 2$

(b) $3 + 2 > 4 = 9 + 3 < 2$

(c) $3 + 2 < 4 \times 9 + 3 < 3$

(d) $3 > 2 > 4 = 18 + 3 < 1$

74. Rearrange the jumbled up letters in their natural sequence and find the odd one out.

(a) LWKA (b) NRU

(c) EPESL (d) UPJM

75. The following questions are based on the information given below :

Data on 450 students, who took an examination in Science, Mathematics and Social Sciences is given below: Number of students who

- Passed in all subjects : 167
- Failed in Science : 191
- Failed in Mathematics : 199
- Failed in Social Science : 175
- Failed in all subjects : 60
- Passed in Science only : 52
- Passed in Mathematics only : 48
- Passed in Social Science only : 62

How many passed in Mathematics and at least one more subject?

(a) 48 (b) 210

(c) 103 (d) 203

76. How many failed in two subjects only?

(a) 162 (b) 152

(c) 100 (d) 52

77. How many passed at least in one subject?

(a) 350 (b) 395

(c) 390 (d) 340

78. If TWELVE is coded as 87, then ELEVEN is coded as

(a) 86 (b) 78

(c) 36 (d) 63

79. If in a certain code language, ORDINARY is written as 12467923, how will the word RADIAN be written in that code language?

(a) 249697 (b) 294967

(c) 294697 (d) 246967

80. What is the name given to material through which light can pass?

(a) Translucent (b) Opaque

(c) Transparent (d) Vitreous

81. John can cover a certain distance in 1 hour and 15 minutes, by covering one-third of the distance at 3 kmph and the rest at 4 kmph. Find the total distance.

(a) 5.5 km (b) 4.5 km

(c) 4 km (d) 6.5 km

82. Who invented the fountain pen?

(a) Birdseyes

(b) Lewis E. Waterman

(c) Dr. Lee de forest

(d) Augsberg

83. Which robotic spacecraft brought solar particles from space?

(a) Genesis (b) Viking

(c) Cygnus (d) Giotto

84. The branch of physics concerned with study of heat is called

(a) Optics

(b) Acoustics

(c) Thermodynamics

(d) Relativity

85. A cloth supervisor rejects 0.09% of the clothes as defective. How many clothes will be examined to reject 18 clothes?

(a) 30000 (b) 20000

(c) 25000 (d) 18000

86. If P stands for ‘+’, Q stands for ‘–’, R stands for ‘×’, then the value of (10 R 4) (4 R 4) Q 6 =

(a) 65 (b) 56

(c) 50 (d) 60

87. Who according to Forbes 2016 list who is the richest person in the world?

(a) Bill Gates

(b) Mark Zuckerberg

(c) Warren Buffet

(d) Mukesh Ambani

88. An Assertion (A) and a Reason (R) are given below.
Assertion (A): Indian President is the head of the State.
Reason (R): Indian Parliament consists of the President, Lok Sabha and Rajya Sabha.
Choose the correct option.
(a) A is true but R is false
(b) A is false but R is true.
(c) Both A and R are true and R is the correct explanation of A.
(d) Both A and R are true but R is not the correct explanation of A.

89. Find correct alternative for Smile : Laugh : Cry
(a) Frown : Anger : Temper
(b) Touch : Catch : Release
(c) Stand : Sleep : Play
(d) Evening : Night : Day

90. Heart is related to Blood in the same way as Lung is related to
(a) Chest (b) Respiration
(c) Air (d) Oxygen

91. What is the type of soil found in Great Northen Plains?
(a) Alluvial soil
(b) Black soil
(c) Red soil
(d) Laterite soil

92. The ratio of spirit and water in two mixture of 20 litre and 36 litre is 3 : 7 and P : Q respectively. Both the mixture are mixed together and the ratio of the spirit and water in the new mixture is 27 : 29. Find P : Q.
(a) 3 : 2 (b) 5 : 7
(c) 7 : 5 (d) 4 : 5

93. Mayanak sells a pen at Rs. 750, and makes a profit of 50%, At what price should he sell the pen so as to make a loss of 50%?
(a) Rs. 275 (b) Rs. 250
(c) Rs. 350 (d) Rs. 225

94. An Assertion (A) and a Reason (R) are given below.
Assertion (A) : Milk production in India is low as compared to other countries of the world.
Reason (R) : The animal rearers in India are poor.
Choose the correct option.
(a) A is true but R is false.
(b) A is false but R is true.
(c) Both A and R are false.
(d) Both A and R are true.

95. Find the value of $73 \times 73 + 42 \times 42 - 2 \times 73 \times 42$.
(a) 961 (b) 676
(c) 981 (d) 861

96. A can complete a piece of work in 10 days, B in 15 days and C in 20 days. A and B worked together for four days and then A was replaced by C. In how many days was the whole work completed?
(a) 16 days (b) 48/7days
(c) 42/7 days (d) 18/7

97. Choose the pair which is related in the same way as the words in first pair from the given choices
Mountain : Height : : ——— : ———
(a) River : Water
(b) Cave : Depth
(c) Valley : Beauty
(d) Moon : Shadow

98. The average age of a team of 29 members is 23 years. If the age of the team leader be included, then the average increases by 2 months. What is the age of the team leader?
(a) 25 (b) 28
(c) 32 (d) 27

99. Find the least number which when divided by 16, 24, 36 and 54 leaves remainders 12, 20, 32 and 50 respectively.
(a) 432 (b) 444
(c) 428 (d) 452

100. Who currently holds the number one position in World Chess rankings?
(a) Sven Magnus Carlsen
(b) Yu Yangyi
(c) Surya Shekhar
(d) Valdimir kramnik

Answer Sheet

1. (c)	**2.** (b)	**3.** (b)	**4.** (b)	**5.** (b)	**6.** (a)	**7.** (a)	**8.** (d)	**9.** (b)	**10.** (d)
11. (c)	**12.** (d)	**13.** (b)	**14.** (a)	**15.** (b)	**16.** (c)	**17.** (b)	**18.** (b)	**19.** (b)	**20.** (a)
21. (d)	**22.** (b)	**23.** (b)	**24.** (a)	**25.** (b)	**26.** (a)	**27.** (a)	**28.** (d)	**29.** (c)	**30.** (c)
31. (c)	**32.** (c)	**33.** (b)	**34.** (c)	**35.** (c)	**36.** (c)	**37.** (d)	**38.** (c)	**39.** (c)	**40.** (c)
41. (c)	**42.** (b)	**43.** (d)	**44.** (b)	**45.** (a)	**46.** (d)	**47.** (b)	**48.** (a)	**49.** (a)	**50.** (d)
51. (d)	**52.** (b)	**53.** (c)	**54.** (b)	**55.** (c)	**56.** (c)	**57.** (a)	**58.** (d)	**59.** (b)	**60.** (b)
61. (a)	**62.** (d)	**63.** (a)	**64.** (c)	**65.** (a)	**66.** (b)	**67.** (b)	**68.** (c)	**69.** (b)	**70.** (b)
71. (c)	**72.** (d)	**73.** (a)	**74.** (c)	**75.** (d)	**76.** (a)	**77.** (c)	**78.** (d)	**79.** (c)	**80.** (c)
81. (b)	**82.** (b)	**83.** (a)	**84.** (c)	**85.** (b)	**86.** (c)	**87.** (a)	**88.** (d)	**89.** (b)	**90.** (d)
91. (a)	**92.** (c)	**93.** (b)	**94.** (a)	**95.** (a)	**96.** (b)	**97.** (b)	**98.** (b)	**99.** (c)	**100.** (a)

Explanations

20. (a) Let the angles are x, $4x$ and $7x$

We know sum of angles of a triangle is 180°. Hence, $x + 4x + 7x = 180°$

$\Rightarrow 12x = 180°$

$x = 180°/12 \Rightarrow 15$

Greatest angle $= 7 \times 15 = 105°$

Smallest angle $= 15°$

Sum of greatest and smallest angle $= 105 + 15 = 120°$

$$\text{Ratio} = \frac{120}{15} = \frac{8}{1} = 8:1$$

24. (a) $\text{Profit percent} = \frac{15}{85} \times 100 = \frac{300}{17}$

$\Rightarrow 17.64\%$

27. (a) Speed of metro train =

$$\frac{\text{Length of train + length of metro station}}{\text{time}}$$

$$\Rightarrow \frac{125+75}{10} \text{ m/sec}$$

$$\Rightarrow \frac{200}{10} \Rightarrow 20 \text{ m/sec}$$

$$\Rightarrow 20 \times \frac{18}{5} = 72 \text{ km/hr}$$

28. (d) $\cos A = \frac{12}{13} = \frac{BC}{AB}$

Here base = 12 & Hypotenuse = 13

Thus, $AC^2 = AB^2 - BC^2$

$\Rightarrow 13^2 - 12^2$

$= 169 - 144 = 25$

$AC = 5$

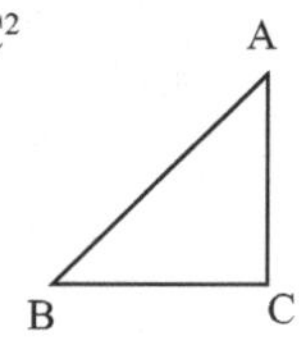

Thus, $\sin A(1 - \tan A)$

$\sin A = \frac{AC}{AB}$ | $\tan A = \frac{AC}{BC}$

$$\Rightarrow \frac{AC}{BC}\left(1 - \frac{AC}{BC}\right)$$

$$\Rightarrow \frac{5}{13}\left(1 - \frac{5}{12}\right)$$

$$\Rightarrow \frac{5}{13}\left(\frac{7}{12}\right) \Rightarrow 35/156$$

34. (c) HCF of 0.32, 2.72, 12.8, 14.4 is 0.16

37. (d) $2^x - 2^{x-1} = 8$

$$\Rightarrow 2^x\left(1 - \frac{1}{2}\right) = 2^3 \Rightarrow 2^x \times \frac{1}{2} = 2^3$$

$2^x = 2^4$

$x = 4$

value of $2x^2 + 4x + 3$

$\Rightarrow 2 \times (4)^2 + 4 \times 4 + 3$

$\Rightarrow 2 \times 16 + 16 + 3$

$\Rightarrow 32 + 16 + 3 = 51$

Latest General Knowledge

❍ **President**	Mr. Ram Nath Kovind
❍ **Vice–president**	Mr. M. Venkaiya Naidu
❍ **Prime Minister**	Mr. Narendra Modi

CENTRAL MINISTRY-2019

Prime Minister–Narendra Modi– Prime Minister and also in-charge of: Personnel, Public Grievances and Pensions; Department of Atomic Energy; Department of Space; and All important policy issues; and All other portfolios not allocated to any Minister.

CABINET MINISTER

Ministry	Minister

- Home Affairs **–Amit Shah**
- External Affairs **–Dr. S. Jaishankar**
- Defence **–Raj Nath Singh**
- Finance and Corporate Affairs **–Nirmala Sitharaman**
- Road Transport and Highways; and Micro, Small and Medium Enterprises **–Nitin Jairam Gadkari**
- Chemicals and Fertilizers **–D.V. Sadananda Gowda**
- Consumer Affairs, Food and Public Distribution **–Ramvilas Paswan**
- Agriculture and Farmers Welfare; Minister of Rural Development; and Minister of Panchayati Raj **–Narendra Singh Tomar**
- Law and Justice; Communications; and Electronics & Information Technology **–Ravi Shankar Prasad**
- Food Processing Industries **–Harsimrat Kaur Badal**
- Social Justice and Empowerment **–Thaawar Chand Gehlot**
- Human Resource Development **–Ramesh Pokhriyal 'Nishank'**
- Tribal Affairs **–Arjun Munda**
- Textiles; Women and Child Development **–Smriti Zubin Irani**
- Health and Family Welfare; Science & Technology; and Minister of Earth Sciences **–Dr. Harsh Vardhan**
- Environment, Forest and Climate Change; and Information & Broadcasting **–Prakash Javadekar**
- Railways; and Minister of Commerce & Industry **–Piyush Goyal**
- Petroleum and Natural Gas; and Minister of Steel **–Dharmendra Pradhan**
- Minority Affairs **–Mukhtar Abbas Naqvi**
- Parliamentary Affairs; Coal; Mines **–Pralhad Joshi**
- Skill Development and Entrepreneurship **–Dr. Mahendra Nath Pandey**
- Heavy Industries and Public Enterprise **–Arvind Ganpat Sawant**
- Animal Husbandry, Dairying and Fisheries **–Giriraj Singh**
- Jal Shakti **–Gajendra Singh Shekhawat**

STATE MINISTERS (INDEPENDENT CHARGE)

Ministry	Minister

- Planning; and Chemicals and Fertilizers **–Rao Inderjit Singh**
- Labour and Employment **–Santosh Kumar Gangwar**
- Ayurveda, Yoga and Naturopathy, Unani, Siddha and Homoeopathy (AYUSH) **–Shripad Yesso Naik**
- Micro, Small and Medium Enterprises **–Giriraj Singh**
- Development of North Eastern Region; Prime Minister's Office; Personnel, Public Grievances and Pensions; Department of Atomic Energy; and Department of Space **–Dr. Jitendra Singh**
- Culture; and Environment, Forest and Climate Change **–Dr. Mahesh Sharma**

- Communications; and Railways **–Manoj Sinha**
- Youth Affairs and Sports; and Information and Broadcasting **–Col. Rajyavardhan Singh Rathore**
- Power; and New and Renewable Energy **–Raj Kumar Singh**
- Housing and Urban Affairs **–Hardeep Singh Puri**
- Tourism; and Electronics and Information Technology **–Alphons Kannanthanam**

STATE MINISTERS

- Finance **–Shiv Pratap Shukla**
- Parliamentary Affairs; and Statistics and Programme Implementation **–Vijay Goel**
- Health and Family Welfare **–Ashwini Kumar Chaubey**
- Women and Child Development; and Minority Affairs **–Virender Kumar**
- Skill Development and Entrepreneurship **–Anantkumar Hegde**
- Agriculture and Farmers Welfare **–Gajendra Singh Shekhawat**
- Human Resource Development; and Water Resources, River Development and Ganga Rejuvenation **–Dr. Satya Pal Singh**
- External Affairs **–General(Retd.) V.K. Singh**
- Finance **–Santosh Kumar Gangwar**
- Health and Family Welfare **–Faggan Singh Kulaste**
- Drinking Water and Sanitation **–S.S. Ahluwalia**
- Social Justice and Empowerment **–Ramdas Athawale**
- Rural Development **–Ram Kripal Yadav**
- Mines; and Coal
- **–Haribhai Parthbhai Chaudhary**
- Micro, Small and Medium Enterprises **–Giriraj Singh**
- Home Affairs **–Hansraj Gangaram Ahir**
- Drinking Water and Sanitation **–Ramesh Chandappa Jigajinagi**
- Railways **–Rajen Gohain**
- Agriculture and Farmers Welfare; and Panchayati Raj **–Parshottam Rupala**
- External Affairs **–M.J. Akbar**
- Human Resource Development **–Upendra Kushwaha**
- Finance; and Shipping **–Radhakrishnan P.**
- Home Affairs **–Kiren Rijiju**
- Social Justice and Empowerment **–Krishan Pal**
- Tribal Affairs **–Jasvantsinh Sumanbhai Bhabhor**
- Steel **–Vishnu Deo Sai**
- Tribal Affairs **–Sudarshan Bhagat**
- Civil Aviation **–Jayant Sinha**
- Heavy Industries and Public Enterprises **–Babul Supriyo**
- Food Processing Industries **–Sadhvi Niranjan Jyoti**
- Social Justice and Empowerment **–Vijay Sampla**
- Parliamentary Affairs; and Water Resources, River Development and Ganga Rejuvenation **–Arjun Ram Meghwal**
- Textiles **–Ajay Tamta**
- Agriculture and Farmers Welfare **–Krishna Raj**
- Road Transport and Highways; Shipping; and Chemicals and Fertilizers **–Mansukh L. Mandaviya**
- Health and Family Welfare **–Anupriya Patel**
- Consumer Affairs, Food and Public Distribution; and Commerce and Industry **–C.R. Chaudhary**
- Law and Justice; and Corporate Affairs **–P.P. Chaudhary**
- Defence **–Subhash Ramrao Bhamre**

DIGNITARIES OF INDIA

- Chief CBI **– Rishi Kumar Shukla**
- Chairman, Air India **– Ashwani Lohani**
- Chief Justice of India**– Justice Ranjan Gogoi**
- Loksabha Speaker **–Om Birla**
- Deputy Chairman, Rajya Sabha **– P. J. Kurian**
- Cabinet Secretary **– Pradip Kumar Sinha**
- Controller and Auditor General **– Rajeev Maharshi**
- Chief Election Commissioner **– Sunil Arora**
- Chairman, UPSC **– Arvind Saxena**
- Air Chief Marshal **– Virendra Singh Dhanoa**
- Navy Admiral **– Karambir Singh**
- Army chief **– Gen. Bipin Rawat**
- Chairman, National Commission for Minorities **– Syed Ghayorul Hasan Rizvi**
- Governor, RBI **– Shakti Kanta Das**
- Chairman, UGC **– Prof. D.P. Singh**
- Chairman, Railway Board **– Vinod Yadav**
- Director, Intelligence Bureau **– Arvind Kumar**
- Chairman, FICCI **– Sandip Somany**
- Chairman, ISRO **– Dr K. Sivan**
- Chairman, Central Direct Tax Board **– Sushil Chandra**
- Chairman, 15th Finance Commission **– N.K. Singh**
- Raw Chief **– Samant Goel**

HEADS OF NATIONAL BANKS

Bank	Managing Director
State Bank of India	Rajnish Kumar (Chairman)
Allahabad Bank	S.S. Mallikarjuna Rao
Bank of Baroda	P. S Jaya Kumar
Bank of India	Dinabandhu Mohapatra
Canara Bank	Rakesh Sharma
Bank of Maharashtra	A.S. Rajeev
Andhra Bank	J. Packirisamy
Corporation Bank	P.V. Bharathi
Indian Bank	Padmaja Chunduru
Dena Bank	Karnam Sekar
Indian Overseas Bank	R. S. Kumar
Oriental Bank of Commerce	Mukesh Kumar Jain
Punjab National Bank	Sunil Mehta
Punjab and Sindh Bank	S. Hari Shanker
Syndicate Bank	Mrutyunjay Mahapatra
Union Bank of India	Rajkiran Rai G
United Bank of India	Ashok K. Pradhan
Vijaya Bank	RA Shankar Narayan
Central Bank of India	Pallav Mahaptra
UCO Bank	Atul Kumar Goel

HEADS OF PRIVATE BANKS

Bank	Managing Director
Dhanlakshmi Bank	T. Latha
Federal Bank	Shyam Srinivasan
Jammu & Kashmir Bank	Parvez Ahmad
Karnataka Bank	MS Mahabaleshwara
Karur Vysya Bank	P.R. Seshadri
Nainital Bank	Mukesh Kumar Sharma (Chairman)
South Indian Bank	V. G. Matthew
Tamilnadu Merchantile Bank	K.V. Ramamoorthy
Catholic Syrian Bank	C.V. R. Rajendran
City Union Bank	N. Kamakodi
Axis Bank	Amitabh Choudhary
HDFC Bank	Aditya Puri
RBL (Ratnakar) Bank Ltd.	Vishwavir Ahuja
Yes Bank	Ravneet Singh Gill
ICICI Bank	Mr. Sandeep Bakhshi
Indusind Bank	Romesh Sobti
IDFC Bank	Dr. Rajiv B. Lall

DIRECTORS OF MAHARATNA COMPANIES

Company	Chairman
Bharat Heavy Electricals Ltd. (BHEL)	Atul Sobti
Coal India Ltd. (CIL)	Anil Kumar Jha
Gas Authority of India Ltd. (GAIL)	B C. Tripathi
Indian Oil Corporation Ltd. (IOC)	Sanjiv Singh
Oil and Natural Gas Corporation Ltd. (ONGC)	Shashi Shanker
Steel Authority of India Ltd. (SAIL)	Anil Kumar Chaudhary
National Thermal Power Corporation Ltd. (NTPC)	Gurdeep Singh
Bharat Petroleum Corporation Limited (BPCL)	D Rajkumar

UNION TERRITORIES AND THEIR ADMINISTRATORS

- Andaman and Nicobar Islands – **Devendra Kumar Joshi**
- Chandigarh – **V. P. Singh Badnor (Admn.)**
- Daman and Diu – **Prafulla Patel (Admn.)**
- Dadra and Nagar Haveli – **Vikram Dev Dutt (Admn.)**
- Delhi – **Anil Baijal (LG)**
- Puducherry – **Kiran Bedi (LG)**
- Lakshadweep – **Farukh Khan (Admn.)**

GOVERNORS AND CHIEF MINISTERS OF THE INDIAN STATES

State	Governor	Chief Minister
Andhra Pradesh	Biswa Bhushan Harichandan	Jagan Mohan Reddy
Arunachal Pradesh	B. D. Mishra	Pema Khandu
Assam	Jagdish Mukhi	Sarbananda Sonowal
Goa	Mridula Sinha	Pramod Sawant
Gujarat	Acharya Dev Vrat	Vijay Rupani
Jammu & Kashmir	Satyapal Malik	(State under Governor's Rule)
Karnataka	Vajubhai Wala	H.D. Kumaraswamy
Kerala	P. Satshivam	Pinarayi Vijayan
Maharashtra	Chennameni Vidyasagar Rao	Devendra Fadanvis
Manipur	Padmanabh Acharya	N. Biren Singh
Meghalaya	Tathagat Rai	Conrad Sangma
Mizoram	Prof. Jagdish Mukhi (Add charge)	Zoramthanga
Nagaland	R. N. Ravi	Neiphu Rio
Odisha	Prof. Ganeshi Lal	Navin Patnayak
Sikkim	Ganga Prasad	Prem Singh Tamang
Tamil Nadu	Banwarilal Purohit	E. K. Palanishwani
Tripura	Ramesh Bains	Biplab Kumar Deb
Uttrakhand	Baby Rani Maurya	Trivendra Singh Rawat
West Bengal	Jagdip Dhankhar	Mamta Banerjee
Rajasthan	Kalyan Singh	Ashok Gehlot
Uttar Pradesh	Aanandi Ben Patel	Aditya Nath Yogi
Bihar	Fagu Chauhan	Nitish Kumar
Punjab	V. P. Singh Badnor	Capt. Amarindra Singh
Delhi	Anil Baizal	Arvind Kejriwal
Himachal Pradesh	Kalraj Mishra	Jai Ram Thakur
Haryana	Satyadev Narayan Arya	Manohar Lal Khattar
Madhya Pradesh	Lalji Tondon	Kamal Nath
Chhatishgarh	Anusuiya Uikey	Bhupesh Baghel
Telangana	E. S. L. Narsimhan (Add charge)	K. Chandrashekhar Rao
Jharkhand	Dropadi Murmu	Raghuvar Das

HEADS OF VARIOUS MILITARY/POLICE DEPARTMENTS OF INDIA

Military/Police Department	Head	Time–Period
Air Force	Air Chief Marshals Virendra Singh Dhanoa	Jan., 2017 – Present
Navy	Vice Admiral Karambir Singh	May, 2019 – Present
Military	General Bipin Rawat	Dec., 2016 – Present

Border Security Force (BSF)	Rajnikant Mishra	Sep., 2018 – Present
ITBP	S. S. Deswal	Nov., 2018 – Present
CRPF	Rajiv Rai Bhatnagar	Feb., 2016 – Present
CISF	Rajesh Ranjan	April, 2018 – Present
Assam Rifles	Lt. Gen Shokin Chauhan	Oct., 2016 – Present
SSB	Kumar Rajesh Chandra	Jan., 2019 – Present
National Security Guard (NSG)	Sudeep Lakhtakia	Feb., 2018 – Present

HEADS OF INTERNATIONAL INSTITUTES/ORGANIZATIONS

Head	Organization	Head	Organization
Antonio Guterres (Portuguese)	• **Secretary General, United Nations Organization (UNO)**	Li Yang (China)	• **Director General, United Nations Industrial Development Organization (UNIDO)**
Miroslav Lajĉâk (Slovakia)	• **Chairman, United Nations General Assembly (UNGA)**	Anthony Lake (USA)	• **Director General, United Nations Child Emergency Fund (UNICEF)**
Yukio Amano (Japan)	• **Director General, International Atomic Energy Agency (IAEA)**	Ronny Abraham (France)	• **Chairman, International Court (ICJ)**
Guy Rider (U.K)	• **Director General, International Labor Organization (ILO)**	Achim Steiner (Brazilian, German)	• **Administrator, United Nations Development Program (UNDP)**
Jose Graziano da Silva (Brazil)	• **Food and Agriculture Organizations (FAO)**	Filippo Grandi (Italy)	• **United Nations High Commissioner for Refugees (UNHCR)**
Audrey Azoulay (French)	• **Director General, United Nation Educational; Scientific and Cultural Organization (UNESCO)**	Mr. Joaquin Alexander Maza Martelli (El Salvador)	• **President, United Nations Human Rights Council (UNHRC)**
Sebastian Coe (Britain)	• **Chairman, International Association of Athletics Federations (IAAF)**	Alpha conde (Guinea)	• **African Union (AU)**
Tedros Adhanom (Ethiopia)	• **Director General, World Health Organization (WHO)**	Dato Lim Jock Hoi (Brunei)	• **Secretary General, ASEAN**
Christine Lagarde (France)	• **Managing Director, International Monetary Fund (IMF)**	Mohammad Saheni Barkindo	• **Secretary General,OPEC**
David Malpass (USA)	• **Chairman, World Bank (WB)**	Amjad Hussain B. Sial (Pakistan)	• **Secretary General, SAARC**
Roberto Azevedo (Brazil))	• **Director General, World Trade Organization (WTO)**	Mahmoud Abbas (Palestine)	• **Chairman, Palestine Liberation Organization (PLO)**
Mukhisa Kituyi (Kenya)	• **Secretary–General of UNCTAD**	Yousef Al-Othaimeen (Saudi Arabia)	• **Secretary General, Organization of Islamic Cooperation (OIC)**

VARIOUS COMMITTEES AND THEIR FIELD OF WORK

Name	Field of Work
Swaminathan Committee	Population Policy
Jankiram Committee	Security Transaction
Dantwala Committee	Estimation of Unemployment
Rekhi Committee	Indirect Tax
Sarkaria Committee	Center–State Relation
Goswami Committee	Industrial sickness
Mahalanobis Committee	National Income
Rangarajan Committee	Balance of Payment,
Raja Chelaiya Committee	Tax Reform
Malhotra Committee	Broad Framework of Insurance Sector
Khusro Committee	Agricultural Credit System
Goiforiya Committee	Improvement In The Customer service At Primary (Urban) Cooperative Banks
Bhurelal Committee	—
Narsinham Committee	Banking Reforms
Bhandari Committee	Restructuring of RRB
Sachchar Committee	Social, Economic and Educational condition of the Muslim Community of India.
Suresh Tendulkar Committee	Measurement of poverty
S. Tarapor Committee	Capital Account Convertibility on Rupees
Abid Hussain Committee	On Small Scale Industries
Dr. Kirit S. Parikh Committee	Pricing of Diesel, Petrol & LPG Products
V. S. Vyas Committee	Committee on Agriculture and Allied Sector
Mahajan Committee (1997)	Sugar Industry
Abhijit Sen Committee (2002)	Long Food Policy
Besal Committee	Banking Supervision
Ajit Kumar Committee	Army Pay Scales
C B. Bhave Committee	Company information
Kelkar Committee	Tax structure reform
Kumar Manglam Birla Report	Corporate Governance
G.V. Ramkrishnan Committee	Disinvestment
J. J.Irani Committee	Company Law Reforms
Malegam Committee	Reforms In The Primary Market & Repositioning of UTI
Chandrashekhar Committee	Venture Capital
Deepak parikh Committee	Unit Trust of India
Justice Verma Committee	Amendments to Criminal Law

PRESIDENTS OF INDIA

Dr. Rajendra Prasad	1950–62
Dr. S. Radhakrishnan	1962–67
Dr. Zakir Hussain	1967–69
V. V. Giri	1969–69
Justice Mohammad Hidayatullah	1969–69
V. V. Giri	1969–74
Fakhruddin Ali Ahmed	1974–77
B. D. Jatti	1977–77
Neelam Sanjeev Reddy	1977–82
Gyani jail Singh	1982–87
R. Venkatraman	1987–92
Dr. Shankar Dayal Sharma	1992–97
k. R. Narayanan	1997–2002
Dr. A. P. J. Abdul Kalam	2002–07
Pratibha Devi Singh Patil	2007–12
Pranab Mukherjee	2012–2017
Ramnath Kovind	2017 – Present

PRIME MINISTERS OF INDIA

Jawahar Lal Nehru	1947–64
Gulzari Lal Nanda	1964–64
Lal Bahadur Shashtri	1964–66
Gulzari Lal Nanda	1966–66
Indira Gandhi	1966–77
Morarji Desai	1977–79
Choudhari Charan Singh	1979–80
Indira Gandhi	1980–84
Rajiv Gandhi	1984–89
V. P. Singh	1989–90
Chandrashekhar	1990–91
P. V. Narsimha Rao	1991–96
Atal Bihari Vajpayee	1996–96
H. D. Devagowda	1996–97
I K. Gujral	1997–98
Atal Bihari Vajpayee	1998–2004
Dr. Manmohan Singh	2004–09
Dr. Manmohan Singh	2009–14
Narendra Modi	2014 – Present

VICE–PRESIDENTS OF INDIA

Dr. Sarvpalli Radhkrishnan	1952–62
Dr. Zakir Hussein	1962–67
V. V. Giri	1967–69
Gopal Swroop Pathak	1969–74
b. D. Jatti	1974–79
Justice Hidayatullah	1979–84
R. Venkatraman	1984–87
Dr. Shankar Dayal Sharma	1987–92
K. R. Narayanan	1992–97
Krishna Kant	1997–2002
Bhairo Singh Shekhawat	2002–07
Dr. Hamid Ansari	2007 – 2017
M. Venkaiya Naidu	2017 – Present

HIGH COURTS OF INDIA

Serial No.	Name of the Court	Estd. Year
1.	Kolkata (Calcutta)	1862
2.	Mumbai (Bombay)	1862
3.	Chennai (Madras)	1862
4.	Allahabad	1866
5.	Karnataka	1884
6.	Patna	1916
7.	Madhya Pradesh	1956
8.	Jammu and Kashmir	1943
9.	Punjab and Haryana	1919
10.	Guwahati	1948
11.	Odisha	1948
12.	Rajasthan	1949
13.	Andhra Pradesh*	2019
14.	Kerala	1956
15.	Gujrat	1960
16.	Delhi	1966
17.	Himachal Pradesh	1971
18.	Sikkim	1975
19.	Chhatisgadh	2000
20.	Uttrakhand	2000
21.	Jharkhand	2000
22.	Manipur	2013
23.	Meghalaya	2013
24.	Tripura	2013
25.	Telangana#	1954

* (After established of high court of Telangana.)

(Formaly known as high court of Andhra Pradesh.)

DISTRIBUTION OF SEATS IN LOK SABHA

State	Seats	State	Seats
Andhra Pradesh	25	Rajasthan	25
Arunachal Pradesh	2	Sikkim	1
Assam	14	Tamil Nadu	39
Uttrakhand	5	Jammu and Kashmir	6
Bihar	40	Karnataka	28
Goa	2	Kerala	20
Gujarat	26	Uttar Pradesh	80
Chhatisgadh	11	West Bengal	42
Jharkhand	14	Madhya Pradesh	29
Haryana	10	Telangana	17
Himachal Pradesh	4	**Union Territories**	
Maharashtra	48	Delhi	7
Manipur	2	Andaman and Nicobar Islands	1
Meghalaya	2	Chandigarh	1
Mizoram	1	Dadar and Nagar Haveli	1
Nagaland	1	Daman and Diu	1
Odisha	21	Lakshdweep	1
Punjab	13	Puducherry	1
Tripura	2	Nominated Anglo Indians	2
			Total = 545

ALLOTMENT OF SEATS IN RAJYA SABHA (FOURTH SCHEDULE)

State	No. of Members	State	No. of Members
Andhra Pradesh	11	Rajasthan	10
Assam	7	Uttar Pradesh	31
Bihar	16	West Bengal	16
Jharkhand	6	Uttrakhand	3
Goa	1	Jammu and Kashmir	4
Gujrat	11	Nagaland	1

Haryana	5	Himachal Pradesh	3
Kerala	9	Manipur	1
Madhya Pradesh	11	Tripura	1
Chhatisgadh	5	Meghalaya	1
Tamil Nadu	18	Sikkim	1
Maharashtra	19	Mizoram	1
Karnataka	12	Arunachal Pradesh	1
Odisha	10	Delhi	3
Punjab	7	Puducherry	1
Nominated Members	12	Telangana	7
			Total = 245

LOK SABHA SPEAKERS

G. V. Mavalankar	1952–56
M. A. Ayangar	1956–62
Hukum Singh	1962–67
Neelam Sanjeev Reddy	1967–69
Gurdayal Singh Dhillon	1969–75
Bali Ram Bhagat	1976–77
Neelam Sanjeev Reddy	1977–77
K. S. Hegde	1077–80
Balram Jakhar	1980–89
Ravi Rai	1989–91
Shivraj V. Patil	1991–96
P. A. Sangma	1996–98
G. M. C. Balyogi	1998–2002
Manohar Joshi	2002–2004
Somnath Banerjee	2004–09
Mira Kumar	2009–2014
Sumitra Mahajan	2014–2019
Om Birla	June 2019 – Present

GOVERNORS OF RESERVE BANK OF INDIA

Osbon Smith	1935–37
James Braid Taylor	1937–43
C. D. Deshmukh	1943–49
Benegal Rama Rao	1949–57
K. G. Ambegaonkar	1957–57
H. V. R. Ayangar	1957–62
P. C. Bhhatacharya	1962–67
L. K. Jha	1967–70
B N. Adarkar	1970–70
S Jaganathan	1970–75
N C. Sen Gupta	1975–75
K R. Puri	1975–77
M Narsimhan	1977–77
Dr. I. G. Patel	1977–82
Dr. Manmohan Singh	1982–85
A Ghosh	1985–85
R N. Malhotra	1985–90
S Venkatraman	1990–92
Dr. C. Rangrajan	1992–97
Dr. Bimal Jalan	1997–2003
Dr. Y. V. Reddy	2003–2008
Dr. D. Subbarao	2008–2013
Raghuram Rajan	2013–2016
Urjit Patel	2016 – 2018
Shakti Kant Das	2018 – Present

COMPTROLLER AND AUDITOR GENERAL

V. Narhari Rao	1948–54
A K. Chanda	1954–60
A K. Rao	1960–66
S Rangnathan	1966–72
A Bakshi	1972–78
Gyan Prakash	1978–84
T N. Chaturvedi	1984–90
C G. Somaiya	1990–96
V K. Shunglu	1996–02
V N. Kaul	2002–08
Vinod Roy	2008–13
Shashikant Sharma	2013 – 2017
Rajiv Mehrishi	2017 – Present

IMPORTANT DAYS OF INDIA

26th January	Republic Day
30th January	Sorrow Day
28th February	National Science Day
3rd March	National Defense Day
4th March	National Security Day
11th May	National Technology Day
26th July	Kargil Victory Day
9th August	Quit India Day

15th August	Independence Day
20th August	Communal Harmony Day
29th August	National Sports Day
5th September	Teacher's Day
2nd October	Gandhi Birth Anniversary
8th October	Indian Air Force Day
10th October	National Postal Day
14th November	Children's Day
4th December	Navy Day
7th December	Armed Forces Flag Day
18th December	Minority Rights Day
23rd December	Farmer's Day

ATTORNEY GENERALS OF INDIA

M. C. Sitalwad	1950–63
C K. Daftari	1963–68
Niran Dey	1968–77
S V. Gupta	1977–79
L N. Sinha	1979–83
K Parasaran	1983–89
Soli J. Sorabji	1989–90
G Ramaswami	1990–92
Milan K. Banerjee	1992–96
Ashok K. Desai	1996–98
Soli J. Sorabji	1998–2004
Milan K. Banerjee	2004–2009
Ghulam E. Vahanvati	2009– June, 2014
Mukul Rohtagi	June 2014– 18 June 2017
K.K. Venugopal	1 July 2017 –Present

IMPORTANT DAYS OF THE WORLD

26th January	International Custom day
4th February	World Cancer Day
20th February	World Social Justice Day
8th March	International Woman's Day
15th March	World Consumer Rights Day
21st March	World Forestry Day
22nd March	World Water day
23rd March	World Weather Science Day
24th March	World T.B Day
7th April	World Health Day
18th April	World Heritage Day
22nd April	Earth Day
23rd April	World Book and Copyright Day
1st May	International Labor Day
3rd May	Freedom of Press Day
8th May	World Red Cross Day
12th May	International Nurse Day
15th May	International Family Day
17th May	World Telecommunication Day
24th May	Commonwealth Day
31st May	Tobacco Prevention Day
5th June	World Environment Day
12th June	World Child Labor Prevention Day
21st June	World Yoga Day
11th July	World Population Day
6th August	Hiroshima Day
9th August	Nagasaki Day
12th August	International Youth Day
19th August	World Photography Day
8th September	World Literacy day
16th September	World Ozone Day
21st September	World Peace Day
27th September	World Tourist Day
1st October	International Day of Older Persons
4th October	World Animal Welfare Day
9th October	World Post Day
16th October	World Food Day
24th October	United Nations Day
14th November	Diabetes Day
1st December	World AIDS Day
10th December	Human Rights Day

FIRST WOMAN IN INDIA

First woman prime minister	Indira Gandhi
First woman Governor in independent India	Sarojini Naidu
First woman ambassador	C B. Muthamma
First woman judge in the Supreme Court	Fatima Bibi

First woman to climb mount Everest	Bachhendri Pal
First woman to climb mount Everest twice	Santosh Yadav
First woman pilot in the Indian Air Force	Harita Kaur Dayal
First graduate woman	Kadambini Ganguly and Chandramukhi Basu (1883)
First woman airline pilot	Durba Banerjee
First woman to win a gold medal in the Asian Games	Kamlijit Sandhu
First woman chairman of United Nations General Assembly	Vijaya Lakshmi Pandit
First woman chairman of UPSC	Rose Million Bethyu
First woman Police Director General	Kanchan Choudhary Bhattacharya
The first and last woman Muslim ruler of India	Razia Sultan
First woman to receive the Ashok Chakra	Neerja Bhanot
First woman awarded with Gyanpith award	Ashapurna Devi
First Nobel laureate woman	Mother Theresa
First woman to be awarded with Bharat Ratna	Indira Gandhi
First woman chief minister of an Indian state	Sucheta Kriplani
First Chief Justice of High Court	Lila Seth (Himachal Pradesh High Court)
First Miss World	Rita Faria
First woman lawyer	Cornelia Sorabji
First woman to be awarded with Lenin Peace Prize	Aruna Asaf Ali
First woman to win a medal at Olympic games	Karnam Malleshvari
The woman with a world record in Power Lifting	Sumita Laha (1989)
First woman astronaut	Kalpana Chawla

AREA, POPULATION AND DECADAL POPULATION GROWTH RATE OF INDIA AND ITS STATES/UNION TERRITORIES

S. No.	India/State/Union Territory	Area Sq. KM	Total Population (2011)			Decadal Growth Rate (2001–11)
			Person	Men	Women	
	India	**3287469**	**1210269573**	**623121843**	**587447730**	**17.7**
1.	Jammu and Kashmir	222236	12541302	6640662	5900640	23.6
2.	Himachal Pradesh	55673	6864602	3481873	3382729	12.9
3.	Punjab	50362	27743338	14639365	13103873	13.9
4.	Chandigarh	114	1055450	580663	474787	17.2
5.	Uttrakhand	53483	10086292	5137773	4948519	18.8
6.	Haryana	44212	25351462	13491734	11856728	19.9
7.	Delhi, N. C. R.	1483	16787941	8987326	7800615	21.2
8.	Rajasthan	342239	68548437	35550997	32997440	21.3
9.	Uttar Pradesh	240928	199812341	104480510	95331831	20.2
10.	Bihar	94163	104099452	54278157	49821295	25.4

11.	Sikkim	7096	610577	323070	287507	12.9
12.	Arunachal Pradesh	83743	1383727	713912	669815	26.0
13.	Nagaland	16579	1978502	1024649	953853	–0.6
14.	Manipur	22327	2570390	1290171	1280219	18.6
15.	Mizoram	21081	1097206	555339	541867	23.18
16.	Tripura	10486	3673917	1874376	1799541	14.5
17.	Meghalaya	22429	2966889	1491832	1475057	27.9
18.	Assam	78438	3120576	15939443	15266133	17.1
19.	West Bengal	88752	91276115	46809027	44467088	13.8
20.	Jharkhand	79716	32988134	16930315	16057819	22.4
21.	Odisha	155707	41974218	21212136	20762082	14.0
22.	Chhatisgadh	135192	25545198	12832895	12712303	22.6
23.	Madhya Pradesh	308252	72626809	37612306	35014503	20.3
24.	Gujrat	196244	60439692	31491260	28948432	19.3
25.	Daman and Diu	111	243227	150301	92946	53.8
26.	Dadra and Nagar Haveli	491	343709	193760	149949	55.9
27.	Maharashtra	307713	112374333	58243056	54131277	16.0
*28.	Andhra Pradesh	275045	84580777	42442146	42138631	11.0
29.	Karnataka	191791	61095297	30966657	30128640	15.6
30.	Goa	3702	1458545	739140	719405	8.2
31.	Lakshdweep	30	64473	33123	31350	6.3
32.	Kerala	38852	33406061	16027412	17378649	4.9
33.	Tamil Nadu	130060	72147030	36137975	36009055	15.6
34.	Puducherry	490	1247953	612511	635442	28.1
35.	Andaman and Nicobar Islands	8249	380581	202871	177710	6.9

Since Telangana was carved of from Andhra Pradesh June 2014, so all of the census 2011 Data of Telangana are given with Andhra Pradesh.

POPULATION DENSITY AND SEX RATIO IN INDIA AND ITS STATES/UNION TERRITORIES

S. No.	India/State/Union Territory	Population Density 2011	Sex Ratio 2011	Infant Population 2011 (0–6 years)	Ratio of Infant in Total Population 2011	Infant Sex Ratio 2011
	India	**382**	**943**	**164478150**	**13.6**	**919**
1.	Jammu and Kashmir	**124**	889	2018905	16.1	862
2.	Himachal Pradesh	**123**	972	777898	11.3	909
3.	Punjab	**551**	895	3076219	11.1	846

4.	Chandigarh	**9258**	818	119434	11.3	880
5.	Uttrakhand	**189**	963	1355814	13.4	890
6.	Haryana	**573**	879	3380721	13.3	834
7.	Delhi, N. C. R.	**11320**	868	2012454	12.0	871
8.	Rajasthan	**200**	928	10649504	15.5	888
9.	Uttar Pradesh	**829**	912	30791331	15.4	902
10.	Bihar	**1106**	918	19133964	18.4	935
11.	Sikkim	**86**	890	64111	10.6	957
12.	Arunachal Pradesh	**17**	938	212138	15.3	972
13.	Nagaland	**119**	931	291071	14.7	943
14.	Manipur	**115**	992	338254	13.2	936
15.	Mizoram	**52**	976	168531	15.4	970
16.	Tripura	**350**	960	458014	12.5	957
17.	Meghalaya	**132**	989	568536	19.2	970
18.	Assam	**398**	958	4638130	14.9	962
19.	West Bengal	**1028**	950	10581466	11.6	956
20.	Jharkhand	**414**	949	5389495	16.3	948
21.	Odisha	**270**	979	5273194	12.6	941
22.	Chhatisgadh	**189**	991	3661689	14.3	969
23.	Madhya Pradesh	**276**	931	10809395	14.9	918
24.	Gujrat	**308**	919	7777262	12.9	890
25.	Daman and Diu	**2191**	618	26934	11.1	904
26.	Dadra and Nagar Haveli	**700**	774	50895	14.8	926
27.	Maharashtra	**365**	929	13326517	11.9	894
*28.	Andhra Pradesh	**308**	993	9142802	10.8	939
29.	Karnataka	**319**	973	7161033	11.7	948
30.	Goa	**394**	973	144611	9.9	942
31.	Lakshdweep	**2149**	947	7255	11.3	911
32.	Kerala	**860**	1084	3472955	10.4	964
33.	Tamil Nadu	**555**	996	7423832	10.3	943
34.	Puducherry	**2547**	1037	132858	10.6	967
35.	Andaman and Nicobar Islands	**46**	876	40878	10.7	968

* Since Telangana was carved out from Andhra Pradesh June 2014, so all of the census 2011 Data of Telangana are given with Andhra Pradesh.

Union Budget 2019-20

Finance Minister Nirmala Sitharaman presented the Union Budget 2019-20 in the Lok Sabha on July 5, 2019 along with the Finance Bill.

☞ Income Tax Slabs of Individual below 60 years of age

Income Slab	Income Tax Rate
Up to Rs 2.5 lakh	Nil
Rs 2. 5 Lakh to Rs 5 Lakh	5% of Total income minus Rs 2,50,000
Rs 5 Lakh to Rs 10 Lakh	Rs 12,500 + 20% of Total income minus Rs 5,00,000
Rs 10 Lakh and above	Rs 1,12,500 + 30% of Total income minus Rs 10,00,000
Income Tax Slabs of individual between 60 and 80 years of age (Senior Citizen)	Nil
Up to Rs 3 lakh	Nil
Rs 3 lakh to Rs 5 lakh	5% of Total income minus Rs 3 lakh
Rs 5 lakh to Rs 10 lakh	Rs 10,000 + 20% of Total income minus Rs 5 lakh
Rs 10 lakh and above	Rs 1,10,000 + 30% of Total income minus Rs 10 lakh
Income Tax Slabs for individuals above 80 years of age (Super Senior Citizen)	Nil
Up to Rs 5 lakh	Nil
Rs 5 lakh to Rs 10 lakh	20% of Total income minus Rs 5 lakh
Rs 10 lakh and above	Rs 1 lakh + 30% of Total income minus Rs 10 lakh

- Surcharge on individuals having taxable income from Rs 2 crore to Rs 5 crore; and 5 crore and above will be enhanced. The effective tax rate will increase by around 3% and 7% respectively.
- Businesses with annual turnover of over Rs 50 crore will offer low-cost digital payments. No charges will be levied on customers and merchants. RBI will bear these expenses.
- Additional income tax deduction of 1.5 lakh rupees on the interest paid on loans taken to purchase e-vehicles.
- Additional deduction upto Rs. 1.5 lakh will be provided to boost affordable housing for interest paid on loans borrowed up to 31st March 2020 for house valued up to Rs. 45 lakh.
- Faceless Income Tax Assessment in electronic mode to be launched in 2019 in a phased manner involving no human interface, to reduce taxpayer trouble.
- Several Direct Tax Incentives to be provided to International Financial Services Centres (IFSCs)
- PAN and Aadhaar made interchangeable for convenience of tax payers; Income Tax returns can now on be filed using Aadhaar number, if PAN card not available and vice-a-versa.
- Levy of TDS of 2 percent on cash withdrawal of more than Rs 1 crore from bank account in a year, to boost digital payments.
- Indian economy to become a $3 Trillion economy in current year (2019-20).
- Government aims to make India a $5 trillion economy.
- **Pension Benefits:** to about 3 crore retail traders & small shopkeepers with annual turnover of less than Rs.1.5 crore.

- For Railway Infrastructure during 2018-2030, Rs.50 lakh crore investments is needed.
- SEBI to consider raising threshold for minimum public shareholding in listed companies from 25% to 35%.
- Insurance Intermediaries to get 100% FDI.
- The statutory limit for FPI investment in a company is suggested to be increased from 24% to sectoral foreign investment limit. Also, option to be given to the concerned corporate to limit it to a lower threshold.
- FPIs to be permitted to subscribe to listed debt securities issued by Real estate investment trusts (REITs) and Infrastructure investment trusts (InvITs).
- NRI-Portfolio Investment Scheme Route is proposed to be merged with FPI Route.
- Cumulative resources garnered through new financial instruments such as InvITs, REITs as well as models like Toll-Operate-Transfer (ToT) exceed Rs. 24,000 crore.
- New Space India Limited (NSIL), a Public Sector Enterpises (PSE), incorporated as a new commercial arm of Department of Space (DoS).

Forest Survey of India-2017

☞ HIGHLIGHTS OF ISFR – 2017

- The Ministry of Environment, Forest and Climate Change (MoEFCC) has released India State of Forest Report (ISFR) 2017. In which total forest **(6778 sq km)** and tree cover **(1243 sq km)** in India has increased of over **8,021 sq km** which is one percent increase from 2015.
- The India State of Forest Report 2017 (ISFR 2017) is **15th** such report in the series prepared by Forest Survey of India (FSI).
- The report has been prepared with the help of scientific tools and contains information on forest cover, tree cover, mangrove cover, carbon stock in India's forests, growing stock inside and outside the forest areas and forest cover in different patch size classes.
- The report for first time contains information on decadal change in water bodies in forest during 2005-2015, forest fire, production of timber from outside forest, state wise carbon stock in different forest types and density classes.
- FSI has been assessing the forest and tree resources of our country on a biennial basis since **1987.** The results of the assessment are published in its biennial report titled "India State of Forest Report (ISFR)"
- The increase in the forest cover has been observed as **6,778 sq** km and that of tree cover as **1,243 sq km.** The total forest and tree cover is 24.39% of geographical area of the country.
- The increase in forest cover has been observed in Very Dense Forest (VDF) which absorbs maximum carbon dioxide from the atmosphere. It is followed by increase in forest cover in open forest.

☞ India's Global Position

- India is ranked 10th in world, with **24.4%** of land area under forest and tree cover, even though it accounts for **2.4 %** of the world surface area and sustains needs of 17 % of human and **18 %** livestock population. India was placed 8th in list of Top Ten nations reporting the greatest annual net gain in forest area.

☞ States/UTs-wise report

- **Top 5 States with maximum increase in forest cover:** Andhra Pradesh (2141 sq km), followed by Karnataka (1101 sq km) and Kerala (1043 sq km), Odisha (885 sq kms) and Telangana (565 sq kms).
- **Top States with maximum Forest cover (in terms of area):** Madhya Pradesh (77,414 sq km) Arunachal Pradesh (66,964 sq km) and Chhattisgarh (55,547 sq km).
- **7 States/UTs have more than 75% forest cover:** Mizoram, Lakshadweep, Andaman & Nicobar Islands, Arunachal Pradesh, Nagaland, Meghalaya and Manipur.
- **15 states/UTs have above 33% of geographical area under forest cover.** About 40% of country's forest cover is present in 9 large contiguous patches of the size of 10, 000 sq.km, or more.
- **8 States/UTs have forest cover between 33% to 75%:** Tripura, Goa, Sikkim, Kerala, Uttarakhand, Dadra & Nagar Haveli, Chhattisgarh and Assam.
- **Top states with highest Forest cover in terms of percentage geographical area:** Lakshadweep with (90.33%), Mizoram (86.27%) and Andaman & Nicobar Islands (81.73%)
- **Top 5 states where forest cover has decreased:** Mizoram (531 sq km), Nagaland (450 sq km), Arunachal Pradesh (190 sq km), Tripura (164 sq km) and Meghalaya (116 sq km). These states are in North Eastern region of the country where total forest cover is very high i.e. more than 70% in each state.
- The main reasons for decrease are shifting cultivation, rotational felling, other biotic pressures, diversion of forest lands for developmental activities, submergence of forest cover, agriculture expansion and natural disasters.

☞ Mangrove cover

- Mangrove eco-systems are rich in biodiversity and provide number of ecological services. They also play a major role in protecting coastal areas from erosion, tidal storms and tsunamis.
- According to ISFR 2017, total mangrove cover stands at **4,921 sq km** and has increased by **181 sq kms. 7 out of 12** mangrove states have shown an increase in mangrove cover and none of them show any negative change.
- **Maharashtra (82 sq kms), Andhra Pradesh (37 sq kms) and Gujarat (33 sq kms)** are top three gainers in terms of mangrove cover.

☞ Water bodies inside forests

- Forests play vital role in water conservation and improve water regime in area.
- According to ISFR 2017, water bodies inside forest cover have increased by **2,647 sq kms** during the last decade. **Maharashtra (432 sq kms), Gujarat (428 sq kms), Madhya Pradesh (389 sq kms)** are top three states showing increase in water bodies within forest areas. Overall, almost all the states have shown a positive change in water bodies.

☞ Bamboo Cover

- The extent of bamboo-bearing area in country is estimated at 15.69 million ha. There has been an increase of 1.73 million ha in bamboo area in compari-son to last assessment done in 2011.
- There is increase of 19 million tonnes in bamboo-growing stock as compared to last assessment done in 2011. The grow-ing stock of bamboo in forest has been estimated to be 189 million tonnes.

Indian Railways At a Glance

- Indian Railways is an Indian state-owned enterprise, owned and operated by the Government of India through the Ministry of Railways. It is one of the world's largest railway networks comprising 115,000 km and 7,112 stations.
- Railways were first introduced to India in the year 1853 from Mumbai to Thane.
- Indian Railways Nationalised in 1951.
- The country's first railway, built by the Great Indian Peninsula Railway.
- The Indian railway system is the largest in Asia and fourth in the world based on rail transport network size after USA, China and Russia.
- It is the biggest employer in the world and the largest single undertaking in the country.
- It has the second biggest electrified system in the world after Russia.
- Indian Railways is divided into 16 zones. Which are further sub-divided into 68 divisions.
- Each zone is headed by a general manager.

RAILWAY ZONES

Name	Established	Headquarters	Divisions
Southern	14 April 1951	Chennai	Chennai, Tiruchirappalli, Madurai and Salem, Palakkad, Thiruvananthapuram
Central	5 November 1951	Mumbai	Mumbai,CST, Bhusawal Pune, Solapur and Nagpur
Western	5 November 1951	Mumbai	Mumbai,Central, Ratlam, Ahmedabad, Rajkot, Bhavnagar and Vadodara
Eastern	14 April 1952	Kolkata	Howrah, Sealdah, Asansol and Malda Town
Northern	14 April 1952	Delhi	Delhi, Ambala, Firozpur, Lucknow and Moradabad
North Eastern	14 April 1952	Gorakhpur	Izzatnagar, Lucknow and Varanasi
South Eastern	1955	Kolkata	Adra, Chakradharpur, Kharagpur and Ranchi
Northeast Frontier	15 January 1958	Maligaon	Alipurduar, Katihar, Rangia, Lumding and Tinsukia
South Central	2 October 1966	Secunderabad	Vijayawada, Secunderabad, Guntakal,Guntur, Hyderabad and Nanded
East Central	1 October 2002	Hajipur	Danapur, Dhanbad, Mughalsarai, Samastipur and Sonpur
North Western	1 October 2002	Jaipur	Jaipur, Ajmer, Bikaner and Jodhpur
East Coast	1 April 2003	Bhubaneswar	Khurda Road, Sambalpur and Visakhapatnam
North Central	1 April 2003	Allahabad	Allahabad, Agra and Jhansi
South East Central	1 April 2003	Bilaspur	Bilaspur, Raipur and Nagpur
South Western	1 April 2003	Hubli	Hubli, Bangalore, Mysore and Gulbarga
West Central	1 April 2003	Jabalpur	Jabalpur, Bhopal and Kota

MANUFACTURING UNIT OF INDIAN RAILWAY

S.No	Name of the Unit	Location
1	Chittaranjan Locomotive Works	Chittaranjan, West Bengal
2	Central Organisation for Railway Electrification	Allahabad, UP
3	Diesel Locomotive Works	Varanasi, UP
4	Diesel Loco Modernisation Works	Patiala, Punjab
5	Integral Coach Factory	Chennai, Tamil Nadu
6	Rail Coach Factory	Kapurthala, Punjab
7	Rail Wheel Factory	Bangalore, Karnataka
8	Rail Coach Factory	Raebareli, UP
9	Rail Wheel Plant	Chhapra, Bihar
10	Diesel Component Factory	Dankuni, West Bengal

ROUTES OF LUXURY TRAINS IN INDIA

S. No	Name	Run by	Route
1	Palace on Wheels	Rajasthan Tourism	Delhi- Jaipur Sawai - Madhopur Chittorgarh-Udaipur Jaisalmer - Jodhpur Bharatpur- Agra -Delhi
2	Deccan Odyssey	Maharashtra Tourism	New Delhi - Sawai Madhopur - Agra -Jaipur - Udaipur -Vadodara - Ellora -Caves - Mumbai
3	The Golden Chariot	Karnataka Tourism	Bengaluru, Kabini, Mysore -Belur Halebidu – Hampi – Badami – Goa – Bengaluru
4	Royal Rajasthan on Wheels	Rajasthan Tourism	Delhi – Jaipur – Jaisalmer – Jodhpur –Sawai – Madhopur – Chittorgarh – Udaipur – Bharatpur – Agra – Delhi

List of committees related to Railways

1. Shahnawaz Committee (1954) - High Level Safety Review Committee
2. Kanjaru Committee (1962) - Railway Accidents Committee
3. Wahchoo Committee (1968) - Railway Safety Committee
4. Seekari Committee (1978) - Railway Accidents Enquiry Committee
5. Khanna Committee (1998) - Railway Safety Review Committee
6. Arvind Panagariya committee (2016) - to fast-track bullet train project

FACTS RELATED TO INDIAN RAILWAYS

- First train in India – Mumbai to Thane, With 400 passengers, this train completed its journey of 34 kms with the help of three engines–Sahib, Sindh and Sultan.
- Father of Indian Railway – Lord Dalhousie
- Fastest train – The Bhopal Shatabdi Express, 1988, between Agra and New Delhi
- Slowest train in India- Nilgri Express,between Chennai and Mettupalayam
- First electric train – Deccan Queen, 1931,connects Mumbai with Pune .
- First double-decker train – Shatabdi train was flagged off in October 2011

- First air-conditioned double-decker train – Shatabdi train will run from Mumbai to Goa
- First underground railway (Metro Railway) – Kolkata Metro(1984)
- Largest Zone in Indian Railways – Northern Railway
- A platform surrounded by rail lines from all the four sides – Island platform
- First railway station – Chhatrapati Shivaji Terminus railway station in Mumbai.
- Longest running train -Vivek Express. It runs from Dibrugarh in upper Assam to Kanyakumari at the southern tip of Tamil Nadu.
- Longest railway platform –Gorakhpur railway station, Uttar Pradesh
- First A.C. Train between Bombay and Baroda started – 1936
- First broad gauge super fast train – Rajdhani express new delhi howrah 1stmarch 1969
- First metre gauge super fast train – pink city express new delhi jaipur 17thoct 1981
- First narrow gauge super fast train – shivalik deluxe express kalka – shimla 9thaug 1996
- First time table 1853 central india
- First stamp on Indian railways 4 annas 10thdec 1936 by king George
- First AC train Mumbai and baroda 1936
- First automatic signalling system 1928
- First railway book stall – 1877 Allahabad wheeler & co ltd
- First wagon in India 1920 Jessop & co., Kolkata
- First vestibules train 1stjune 1930, Deccan queen
- World's first double decker train – 1862 bb&cir
- First railway tunnel of Indian railway -Parsik tunnel
- First rail minister after independence – John Mathai and before independence Asif Ali
- Countries there is no railway line – Lebanon,Mauritius reunion, Libya, Argentina, Afghanistan, Papua,New Guinea
- Trains that have placed in Guinness Book -Darjeeling Toy Train, Nilgiri Mountain Train Simla Toy Train, Mathenron Toy Train, Place on wheels Royal Orient, Buddha circular Express, Fairy Queen.
- Satpura Express numerical name 10001/10002 – run between Jabalpur and Balaghat
- Longest train -Prayagraj Express (26 Coaches, New Delhi–Allahabad)
- Highest Railway station in India – Similiguda (996.08 mt from sea level in the Valtair division of Southern–Eastern Railway)
- Highest river bridge manufactured under Konkan Railway – Panval River Rail bridge (64 mt. high)
- Division that has maximum number of tunnels – Kalka Simla division of Northern Railway (103 tunnels)
- Longest railway bridge of Indian railway – Railway bridge in Kerala near Kochchi joins Idapalli to Vallerpadma (Length 4.62 km)
- Last railway station of Northern Railway and Indian Railway – Bajalta
- Indian state has maximum rail routes – Uttar Pradesh
- Himsagar Express passes through – 11 States(Jammu and Kashmir, Punjab, Haryana, Delhi, Uttar Pradesh, Rajasthan, Madhya Pradesh, Andhra Pradesh, Tamilnadu, Karnataka and Kerala)
- Railway station that has all the three rails -Dumdum Railway station (EMU rail service circular Railway and Metro Railway)
- Railway station has smallest name from the English alphabets -IB (Between Howrah–Nagpur)
- Railway station has longest name –

Venkatanarsimharajuvaripeta (Tamilnadu)

- First female operator in Delhi Metro – Minakshi Sharma.
- First female to become the member of Railway Board – Vijaylaxmi Vishwanathan
- Longest platform situated – Khadagpur (West Bengal)
- Train only for women run – From Churchgate to Boriwali in Mumbai
- Metro Rail in Calcutta – 1984
- Railway week celebrated on 10–16April.
- 19 Railway Recruitment Boards are there in India
- First tourist rail – Palace on wheels in 1982 between Delhi–Jaipur
- Railway accident in the history of Indian Railway occurred in Morghat (Pure–Bombay root) on 5 January, 1869
- Longest rail route in India – from Dibrugarh (Assam) To Kanyakumari
- First monorail operate in India – From Sarhind to Alampur and Bhawani mandi to Patiala
- India's first indigenous steam engine – F–734
- First longest railway tunnel situated between Monkey hill and Khandala (2100 mt)
- First telecommunication between guard and driver – Mumbai–New Delhi (Rajdhani Express)
- First Rajdhani Express ran between New Delhi–Howrah , 1969
- First DC electrical rail engine – Lokmanya (CLW manufactured it in 1961)
- First computer reservation system start in New Delhi, 2002
- Biggest railway yard located in India-Itarasi (Madhya Pradesh)
- Southern Eastern Railway is known as 'Blue chip'
- Metroman – Shridharan (Delhi Metro Rail Engineers)
- First Duranto Express ran between Sialdah and New Delhi 18 September, 2009
- Numbers of Indian railway used to be of 5 Digits from 20 December, 2010
- Busiest railway station in Indian-Lucknow (64 Trains everyday).
- First railway factory established in Jamalpur, 1890
- Train runs between India and Pakistan – Samjhauta Express, Thar Express
- Railway zone launched first Railway Time Table -Central Railway
- State with minimum rail routes – Manipur
- First blind friendly train, from Mysuru to Varanasi – Train no. 16226/ 16230.
- The South Central Railway (SCR) Headquartered in Sikhandrabad has become the first Railway Zone out of Sixteen Railway Zone in the country to complete hundred percent LED Lighting at its all 733 stations.

PHYSICS

Unit

Unit: The measurement index of a quantity is called unit.

Units are of two kind: fundamental unit and derived unit.

Kilogram, meter, candela, second, ampere Kalvin and mole are fundamental units.

1 Light Year = 9.46×10^{15} meter

The biggest unit of distance is Parsec.

1 Parsec = 3.26 Light Years = 3.08×10^{16} m

In the C.G.S system the unit of force is Dyne and in S.I system the unit of force is Newton. 1 newton = 10^5 Dyne.

In the C.G.S system the unit of work done is Erg and in the S.I system the unit is Joule. 1 Joule = 10^7 Erg

Work, Power and Energy

Work is equal to the multiplication of force and the displacement of the object in the direction of the force. Work = Force × Displacement of the object in the direction of force

The rate of work done is called Power. Power is a scalar quantity, its unit of measurement if Watt.

1 Watt hour = 3600 Joules

1 Kilo Watt hour = 3.6×10^6 Joules

1 Horse Power = 746 Watts

An object's capacity to perform a task is called the energy of that object. Energy is a scalar quantity, its unit of measurement is Joule.

- The body that circulates around a planet is called the **satellite** of that planet.

Motion

- **Scalar quantity**: A physical quantity that has magnitude but no direction. E. g. motion, work etc.
- **Vector quantity**: A physical quantity that has magnitude as well as direction of movement. It is added through rules of addition.
- **Distance**: The length traveled by an object in a given time is called Distance. It is always +ve.
- **Displacement**: The horizontal (minimum) distance between two objects in a certain direction.
- **Motion**: The distance covered by an object per second. Its S.I unit is M/S^2
- **Velocity**: The rate of displacement of an object or the distance traveled by an object in a certain direction per second. Its S.I unit is M/S
- **Acceleration**: The rate of change in the velocity of an object. Its S.I unit is M/S^2
- **Angular Velocity**: If a particle is circling around a center then the line that joins that particle to the center makes an angle. The angle that lines makes in a second is called the Angular Velocity of that particle. Linear Motion = Angular Motion × Radius

Isaac Newton, the Father of Physics, propagated the laws motion for the first time in his book **'Principia.'**

First Law: an object will remain at rest or in uniform motion in a straight line unless acted upon by an external force. This law is also called the **Law of Galileo or the Law of Inertia.**

Second Law: the acceleration of an object as produced by a net force is directly proportional to the magnitude of the net force, in the same direction as the net force and inversely proportional to the mass of the object.

Third Law: for every action there is an equal and opposite reaction.

The tendency of an object to remain static or to maintain constant motion in absence of an external force is called **Inertia.**

Gravity

- The force that attracts a body towards any other body having mass is called Gravity.
- Gravity is the force by which the earth pulls the objects toward its center.
- The scale of Gravitational Acceleration (g) on moon is 1/6th of the Gravitational Acceleration of the earth.

$$G = 6.67 \times 10^{-11} \frac{Nm^2}{Kg^2}$$

$$g = 9.8 m/s^2$$

- If a simple pendulum is to be taken to the moon from the earth its periodic season increases because the moon has less Gravitational Acceleration.
- The acceleration that is generated due to gravity is called Gravitational Acceleration (g). Its value is **$9.8M/S^2$**
- Moon is the natural satellite of the earth.
- The orbital motion of a satellite does not depend on its mass. The motion of satellites with varying masses will be the same in the orbit of a radius.
- The orbital motion of a satellite depends on the orbital radius. The orbital motion of a satellite circling close to the earth's surface is estimated to be 7.9 or 8 KM/S.
- The orbital period of the satellite circling close to the earth's surface is 84 minutes.
- Geostationary satellites circle around the earth from a distance of 36000 KM for the earth's surface.
- This satellite orbits along the axis of the earth from west to east and its rotational period is equal to the rotational period of the earth, i.e. 24 hours

The Escape Velocity is the minimum speed needed for an object to break free from the gravity of earth. Once the objects reaches beyond the gravity of earth, it does not return back. Its value is 11.2 KM/S on the surface of the earth.

Escape Velocity is $\sqrt{2}$ times of the orbital velocity.

The Escape Velocity on the moon is 2.38 KM/S, this is why there is no atmosphere on the moon.

Archimedes' Principle

When an object is dipped into liquid, its weight decreases. This illusionary decrease is equal to the mass of the liquid displaced by the object.

Density

- Mass per unit volume is called Density.
- Relative density is measured with hydrometer.
- The density of the ocean water is more than that of the clean water.

Surface Tension

- If liquid's temperature is increased, the surface tension decreases and critical temperature becomes zero.
- The unit of surface tension id Newton/M.
- The surface tension of clean water is higher than that of the soapy water. The surface tension of soapy water can be reduced by mixing it with clean water.
- The force that attracts different atoms of a substance is called Cohesive Force. Whereas the force that attracts the atoms of different substances is called Adhesive Force.
- It is because of the Adhesive Force that water drenches other things and mercury does not attach to glass.

Capillary Action

The process by which the liquid goes up or down in a test tube is called Capillary Action.

Counterforce

The force applied at per unit area is called Counterforce. Its unit is Newton m^2 or Pascal.

Deformity

The change in shape or size of an object is called Deformity.

The ratio of counterforce and deformity is called Elasticity Multiple.

If the deformity and the counterforce is longitudinal, then the Elasticity Multiple is called **Young Elasticity Multiple.**

According to snell's law when a light ray passes from one medium to another

the angle of incidence to the angle of refraction is constant

Pressure

The force applied at per unit area of a surface is called Pressure.

Its unit is Newton/M^2. It is a vector quantity.

Atmospheric pressure is measured with a **Barometer.**

Hydraulic lift, hydraulic press and hydraulic brake etc. are based on **Pascal's Law.**

The melting point of an object increases as the pressure increases.

The objects whose volume decreases after heating, their melting point also decreases under pressure.

The boiling point of all the liquids increases as the pressure decreases.

Bernoulli's Theorem

- When a liquid flows inside a test tube in a linear motion, then the total of energy (pressure energy; static energy and kinetic energy) pressure at its volume remains constant on every point of its journey.
- Venturimeter, Bunsen burner, carbon filter pump, Magnus effect and the speed of the aeroplane are based on Bernoulli's Theorem.

Simple Pendulum

A spherule hanged with a cord attached to a firm base is called a Simple Pendulum.

The rotation period T= $2\pi\sqrt{\frac{l}{g}}$

The maximum rotational period of the pendulum is 84.6 minutes.

Wave

- Wave is an oscillation that transfers energy from one place to another.
- Wave are of two types: 1) Mechanical Waves (Longitudinal Waves and Transverse Waves) and 2) Electro-Magnetic Waves

Types of Waves

- **Longitudinal Waves:** particles of the medium are displaced in a direction parallel to the direction of energy transport. Sound waves are an example of longitudinal waves.
- **Transverse Waves:** particles of the medium are displaced in a direction perpendicular to the direction of energy transport. Waves generated on the surface of the water and light waves are examples of transverse waves.
- **Electro-Magnetic Waves:** these waves do not require a medium for travelling. Light and heat are examples of electro-magnetic waves. These waves travel with the speed of light.

Sound Waves

- Sound travels from one place to another in the form of waves.
- Sound waves are **longitudinal waves.**
- Sound waves have mainly three frequency ranges:

1. **Audible Waves:** the waves between the ranges of **20 Hertz to 20000 Hertz** are called Audible Waves. We can listen to these waves with our ears.
2. **Infrasonic Waves:** the sound waves below the range of 20 Hertz are called Infrasonic Waves. We cannot listen to these waves with our ears.
3. **Ultrasonic Waves:** the sound wave with the range of over 20000 Hertz are called Ultrasonic Waves. Human ears cannot listen these waves but cats, dogs and mosquitos can listen to these waves. Bats can even produce these waves.

The Use of Ultrasonic Waves:

1. Sending signals
2. Measurement of sea level

3. Repairing of expensive clothes, airplane and watch parts.
4. Cleaning the chimneys of factories
5. Destroying the pathogens in milk
6. Helps bats to navigate in darkness
7. Curing arthritis and detection of brain tumor

Heat

- ♦ Heat is an energy that makes us feel the warmth of objects.
- ♦ Its unit is Calorie, Kilo Calorie and Jules.
- ♦ 1 calories = 4.186 Jules

Temperature

- ♦ Temperature is the measurement of warmth and coldness of an object.
- ♦ Thermometer is used to measure the temperature.
- ♦ The average temperature of human body is 37°c or 98.4°F
- ♦ °C and °F become equal at -40°c
- ♦ The medical thermometer measures temperature from 96°F to110°F.

$$\frac{C}{5} = \frac{F-32}{9} = \frac{R}{4} = \frac{K-273}{5} = \frac{Ra-49.2}{9}$$

- ♦ The freezing point of mercury is -39°c and the freezing point of alcohol is -25°c.

Specific Heat

- ♦ Specific heat is the amount of heat that causes a specific amount of heat in the per unit mass of an object.
- ♦ Its unit is Jules or KG Kalvin.
- ♦ Water has the highest specific heat.
- ♦ Most of the objects register increase in specific heat as the temperature increases.
- ♦ The specific heat of water decreases until the temperature rises from 0°c to 40°c. After this point, its specific heat increases.
- ♦ The specific heat of water at 15°c is 4180Jules/ KG–Kalvin.
- ♦ Mercury has low specific heat.
- ♦ The specific heat of gold is 130 Jules/KG Kalvin.

Latent Heat

- ♦ Latent heat is energy released or absorbed by a body during a constant temperature process that is specified in some way.
- ♦ The melting latent heat of ice is 80 Jules/KG **Kalvin**.
- ♦ The latent heat of evaporation is 540 Calorie/ Gram.

Heat Transferring

- ♦ The process of the heat traveling from one place to another is called heat Transferring.
- ♦ In solid objects, heat transfers through Conduction Process.
- ♦ In liquid and gaseous objects, heat transfers through Convection Process.
- ♦ The reaches to earth from the sun through Convection Process.

Light

Light is a type of energy that travels in the form of electro-magnetic waves. Light is a Transverse Wave.

Ole Rammer measured the speed of light for the first time. Light travels faster in air and vacuum ($3\times10.^{8}$ M/S).

The sunlight reaches to earth in 8 minutes and 19 seconds.

The process when light collides with a shiny surface and turns back is called Reflection.

Incident ray is perpendicular to Incident Point. Incident ray and Reflected ray fall on the same platform. The Angle of Incidence is always equal to the angle of Reflection.

Reflection from a Plane Mirror

- ♦ Reflection is always proportional and inverse to the assumed object.
- ♦ If a person walks toward a mirror with v motion then she will feel her reflection to be moving toward her with a speed of 2v.
- ♦ To see the full reflection of an object in a plane mirror, the height of the mirror should be half of that of the height of the object.
- ♦ The number of reflections formed by plane

mirrors: $n = \left(\frac{360°}{\theta} - 1\right)$

Spherical Mirror

- Spherical mirrors are of two type: concave mirror and convex mirror.
- The reflection formed by convex mirror is smaller, straight and virtual than the object whereas the reflection formed by the concave mirror is bigger and real.

Uses of Concave Mirror

- Shaving 2. Used by the ENT doctors 3. Used in motor vehicle headlights 4. In solar cooker

Uses of Convex Mirror

- The rear-view mirror in the vehicles 2. In sodium reflective lamps

Refraction of Light

- When the light ray travels from one medium to another then its trajectory changes its angle. This change in angle is called Refraction.
- The refraction point of red color is lowest and refraction point of violet color is highest.
- When a light ray travels from one medium to another, its frequency remains unchanged while its wavelength and speed changes.

$$\text{Absolute Refractory Point} = \frac{\text{the speed of light in vaccume}}{\text{the speed of light in}}$$

- Generally, refractory point decreases even while the temperature increases.

Photon Theory of Light: light energy travels in small pockets or bundles, these are called Photon.

Lens

- Lens are of two type: convex lens and conclave lens.
- When a lens is dipped into liquid with higher refractory point, its focal length increases and convex lens starts to behave like conclave lens and conclave lens starts to behave like convex lens. Air bubble acts like conclave lens in liquid.

Human Eye: Minimum range of vision is 25 C.M.

Vision Deformities

- **Myopia:** The person afflicted with this deformity can see the nearby objects but cannot see the distant objects. Concave lens is used to help the person see the distant objects.
- **Hypermetropia:** The person afflicted with this disease cannot see the nearby objects. Convex lens is used to cure this deformity.
- **Presbyopia:** The person becomes unable to see the objects both near and distant. Bifocal lens are used to cure this disease.
- **Astigmatism:** The eye can see horizontally but cannot see vertically. Cylindrical lens are used to cure this illness.

The Speed of Light in Various Mediums

Medium	Speed of Light
Vacuum	3×10^8
Glass	2×10^8
Water	2.25×10^8
Rock Salt	1.96×10^8
Turpentine Oil	2.04×10^8
Nylon	1.96×10^8

Charge

- When two matters are rubbed to with each-other then the charge that is produced is called Static Electric Charge.
- **Benjamin Franklin** defined two types of charges: Positive Charge and Negative Charge.
- The charges of same type **retract** while the opposite charges **attract** each other.
- The magnetic field inside a hollow conductor is **zero.**
- **Conductor:** The matter through which the charge can travel easily is called a Conductor. I. e. silver, copper, aluminum etc.
- **Non-Conductor:** The matters through whom the charge cannot travel are called Non-Conductors. I. e. wood, rubber, paper etc.

Electric Current

- The rate of flow of electric charge in conductor is called an Electric Current. Its unit is Ampere. It is a Vector quantity.

> **Ohm's Law**
>
> The potential difference (voltage) across an ideal conductor is proportional to the current through it.
>
> $I = \frac{V}{R}$ where is R is resistance

- In metals, the resistance increases as the temperature increases.
- In semi-conductors, the resistance decreases as the temperature increases.
- In Electric Decompositions, the resistance decreases as the temperature increases.
- The Specific Resistance of the metals depends entirely on their matter.
- If a cord is stretched and its length is doubled, then its resistance changes but its Specific Resistance remains constant.
- The reverse of the Specific Resistance of a conductor is called Conductivity. Its unit is $(\text{Ohm Meter})^1$.
- **Ammeter:** Is the instrument used to measure electric current. It is always arranged in sequential form. The resistance of ideal ammeter is zero.
- **Voltmeter:** Is an instrument used to measure electronic potential in volts. It is always placed in the circuit parallel order. The resistance of an ideal Voltmeter is infinite.
- **Electric Fuse:** it is an electric safety device used to ensure safety of the instruments attached to an electric circuit. It is made from the alloy of tin and glass. Its melting point is low. It is always attached in the circuit in graded form.
- The filaments of electric bulbs is made of **tungsten**. Its melting point is 3110°c.
- Electric fuses are made with metals with low melting point and so that it can melt and break the circuit if electricity flow increases instantly.
- All the instruments are attached in parallel path in the domestic circuit.

Magnet

- Magnet is made of iron and other matters, it attracts iron and when hanged with a cord it always positions itself into the direction of **North and South Pole.**
- The tip that faces the North Pole is called the North Pole of the magnet and the tip that faces the South Pole is called the South Pole of the magnet.
- The same Poles retract while the opposite Poles attract each-other.

Cathode Rays

- Cathode rays were discovered by **Sir William Cook.**
- They travel in a straight line and shine.
- Cathode rays can penetrate though a thin metal sheet.
- Their speed is 1/10th of the speed of light.

Positive or Canal Rays

- Canal Rays were discovered by Eugen Goldstein.
- Canal rays are formed of positively charged particles.
- They travel in straight line and can deposit themselves in magnetic or electrical field.

They ionize the gases

Particle	Mass (KG)	Charge (Coulomb)	Discoverer
Proton	1.672×10^{-27}	$+1.6 \times 10^{-19}$	Eugen Goldstein
Neutron	1.675×10^{-27}	0	James Chadwick
Electron	9.108×10^{-31}	-1.6×10^{-19}	J. J. Thomson

X-Rays

- These are electromagnetic waves, their wavelength range is 0.1A-100A.
- X-rays were discovered by Wilhelm Rontgen.
- X-rays travel in a straight line.
- They are responsible for the occurrence of reflection, refraction, diffraction and polarization etc.
- These rays do not get deposited in the magnetic or electric field. X-rays reflect the light electricity (Photoelectric) effect.

The use of X-Rays

- **In surgery:** X-rays are used to identify broken bones, bullets and stone etc.
- **In radiography:** X-rays are used as the curatives of some diseases. For example, X-rays are used to destroy the cancerous cells.
- **In spying:** these rays can detect hidden objects inside the human body.
- **In engineering:** X-rays are used to detect cracks or bubbles inside the steel beams in the buildings and bridges.
- **In business:** X-rays are used to detect the difference between true and false diamonds and in identifying the pearl inside the oyster.

Radioactivity

- Radioactivity was discovered by **Antoine Henri Becquerel, Marie Curie and Pierre Curie.** These three were awarded joint Nobel Prize for this discovery.
- The nucleus that contains 83 or more protons are unstable. The nuclei start to emit Alpha (α), Beta (β) and Gamma (γ) rays to gain stability. These nuclei are called radioactive.
- Pierre Curie and his wife Marie Curie discovered a new radioactive element – radium.
- All natural radioactive elements turn into glass after emanating α, β and γ rays.

Nuclear Reactor

- Nuclear Reactor is a process by which the energy generated by nuclear diffusion is converted into electrical energy.
- Uranium -235 or Plutonium -239 is used as fuel in the reactor.
- **Cadmium or Boron** Rod is used is controller in the reactor.

Particle	Mass	Charge	Discoverer	Specialty
Positron	9.108×10^{-27}	$+1.6 \times 10^{-19}$	Carl David Anderson	Anti-particle of electron
Neutrino	0	0	Wolfgang Pauli	
Pi-Mason	274 time of electron	Both positive and negative	Yukawa	Unstable, life span is 10^{-8} seconds
Photon	0	0	Einstein	Its motion is equal to the motion of light

The Specialties of α, β and γ Rays			
Specialty	α	β	γ
Origin	From nucleus	From nucleus	From nucleus
Nature	Positive	Negative	Neutral
Composition	${}_2He^4$	${}_{-1}e^0$	Photon
Mass	6.6×10^{-27}kg	9.1×10^{-31}kg	Zero
Charge	+2e	-1.6×10^{-19}C	Zero
Effect on photographic plate	✓	✓	✓
Effect on electric and magnetic field	✓	✓	

Chemistry

Matter

Something that occupies place, has mass and resists any change in its composition is called Matter.

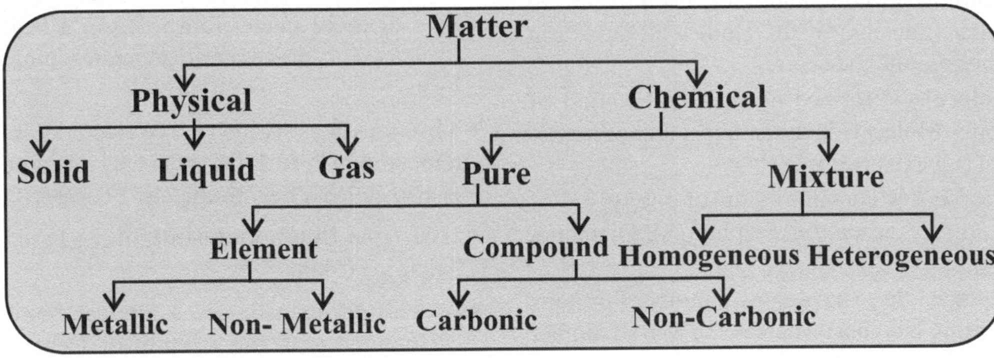

Physical and Chemical Transformations

- The transformations that affect the physical composition of the matter like its color, solidness, density, melting point etc. but does affect its chemical composition chemical properties are called **Physical Transformations.**
- Crystallization, sublimation, boiling, thawing, vaporization, cutting the trees, dissolving of sugar, salt etc. in water are examples of Physical Transformation.
- **Chemical Transformations** affect the chemical composition and chemical properties of the matter, a new matter is formed due to these transformations.
- Burning of fuel, candle, paper, decomposition of water, ripening of fruits etc. are examples of Chemical Transformation.

Different Techniques of Separating a Mixture
1. Crystallization
2. Distillation
3. Sublimation
4. Fractional Distillation
5. Chromatography
6. Steam Distillation

Boiling Point

- The temperature at which the aqueous tension of a liquid becomes equal to the atmospheric pressure is called the **boiling Point** of that liquid.
- **The boiling point increases in the presence of impurities**, hence the boiling point of the oceanic water is higher than that of the pure water.
- As one goes higher in the atmosphere, the atmospheric pressure decreases compared to the sea-level atmospheric pressure.
- Pressure Cooker has higher pressure. This increases the boiling point of the water and the food cooks faster.
- As one goes high up the atmosphere, the atmospheric pressure is less than the air pressure in our lungs. This causes difficulty in breathing.

Melting Point: the temperature at which the solid matter starts to melt into liquid is called the Melting Point of that matter.
Freezing Point: the temperature at which the liquid matter starts to freeze is called the Freezing Point of that matter.

Atom, Molecule and Matter

- Atom is the smallest unit of a matter, it participates in the chemical reactions but it cannot exist in a free state.
- Atoms are made of electrons, protons and neutrons. Protons and neutrons stay in the center (nucleus) of the atom while electron orbits around the center.
- **Molecule** is formed by the combination of atoms. Molecule is the smallest unit of matter that can exist in a free state.
- **The Matter** contains atoms of one type. For example, Carbon (C), Sulphur (S), Diamond, Graphite etc.
- **Isotopes:** these have same number of protons (Atomic Number) whereas the Mass Number (Atomic Number + Number of Neutrons) is variable. Example: H^1, H^2, H^3 etc.
- Isobars: Mass number is constant while Atomic Number varies. Example: ${}_{18}Ar^{40}$, ${}_{19}K^{40}$, ${}_{20}Ca^{40}$ etc.
- Isotone: these have same number of neutrons. For example, ${}_{1}H^3$ and ${}_{2}He^4$ have same number of neutrons in their nucleus.
- **Isoelectronic:** The ions and atoms that have same electronic arrangement. For example, **Ne, Na^+, Mg^{++} $A1^{+++}$** etc.

> **Pauli's Exclusion Principle:** no two electrons in an atom can have identical quantum numbers.
>
> **Hund's Rule** of Maximum Multiplicity: electrons do not form pairs as long as they have empty space to available, in other words – electrons prefer to stay unpaired.
>
> **Heisenberg's Uncertainty Principle:** it is impossible to know simultaneously the exact position and momentum of a particle.
>
> **Aufbau Principle:** the order of writing the increasing energy of atomic brackets in writing the electronic arrangement is as follows:
>
> $1s < 2s < 2p < 3s < 3p < 4s < 3d < 4p < 5s < 4d < 5p < 6s < 4f < 5d < 6p < 7s$

Nuclear Fission

- It is the process by which a heavy nucleus breaks into two or more medium sized nucleus. This process produce immense heat and neutrons.
- Nuclear bomb works on the principle of uncontrolled chain fission. It uses **^{234}Pu** as fuel.

Nuclear Fusion

- Two or more nuclei join to form a heavier nucleus. This process also generates immense heat.
- This process requires extremely high temperature **($>10^6$K)**. That is why this process is also called **Thermonuclear Process.**
- **Hydrogen Bomb and sunlight** are based on Nuclear Fusion.
- In the hydrogen bomb, a nuclear bomb is surrounded with the mixture of Deuterium Oxide **(D_2O)** and Tritium Oxide **(T_2O).**
- **Graham's Rule of Gas Diffusion:**

$$\frac{r_1}{r_2} = \sqrt{\frac{D_2}{D_1}} = \sqrt{\frac{m_2}{m_1}}$$

- The Russian scientist **D. I. Mendeleev's** gave a law after the study of elements and their mixtures gave a law. That law is called **Mendeleev's Periodic Law.** The modern periodic table is based on the law of **Henry Moseley**. In his periodic table the elements are arranged columns and rows according to increasing atomic numbers.

Property	Up to Down	Left to Right
Size of atom	Increases	Decreases
Electro +Ve	Increases	Decreases
Ionized energy	Decreases	Increases
Electro -VE	Decreases	Increases
Electron affinity	Decreases	Increases

- **Radiocarbon method is used to determine the age of elements. Uranium Dating is used to determine the age of the earth, minerals and rocks.**

Acid, Base and Salt

- **Acid** are the mixture elements that contain hydrogen as replacement.

Boyle's Law: For a fixed amount of an ideal gas kept at a fixed temperature, pressure and volume are inversely proportional.

Charles' Law: when the pressure on a sample of a dry gas is held constant, the Kelvin temperature and the volume will be directly proportional.(**T = 273° + t°C**)

Avogadro's Law: equal volumes of all gases, at the same temperature and pressure, have the same number of molecules. At normal temperature and pressure, the volume of 1 gram of any gas is 22.4 liters and this 1 liter contains **6.022×10^{23}** molecules.

- **According to Arrhenius,** acid is a mixture that gives **H^+** ion after dissolving in water.
- According to **Louis Electronic Theory**, acid is a matter that has the tendency to accept the pair of electrons.
- **Aqua Regia:** A mixture in the ratio of 3:1 of concentrated hydrochloric acid and nitric acid. It can melt gold or platinum.
- **Base:** The mixture that provides salt and water after reacting with acid. According to the theory proposed Bronsted Lowry, the element that is capable of accepting protons is called Base. According to Louis Electronic Theory, the element that has the capacity to donate a pair of electrons is Base.
- **Salt:** Salt and water are produced as a result of the reaction between acid and base.
- **pH Scale:** pH scale is used to measure the acid and base content in a solution.
- **Solution:** Is a homogenous mixture of two or more matters in which the relative quantities of the soluble and solvent can go under constant change at a certain temperature.
- **Soluble and Solvent:** In a solution the matter that is present in higher quantity is called the Solvent and the matter in low quantity is called Soluble.
- **Dispersion:** when the particles of one matter are dispersed around another matter, this process is called Dispersion.
- **Suspension:** in this process the size of the dispersed particles is from **$10^{(-3)}$** CM to **$10^{(-4)}$** CM or bigger. These particles can be seen from naked eye. These particles are temporary and are prone to deviate from dispersal medium.

Saturated Solution: A solution made at a certain temperature that has absorbed the maximum possible quantity of the soluble is called a Saturated Solution.

Unsaturated Solution: A solution made at a certain temperature that has the potential of absorbing more soluble at the same temperature is called Unsaturated Solution.

Super Saturated Solution: A Saturated Solution that has the soluble in amount more than what was actually needed to make the solution saturated is called Super Saturated Solution.

Colloid

- Colloid is a heterogeneous solution. It has two phases: Dispersed Phase and Dispersion Medium.
- They reflect solution, Tindall Effect (dispersal of light by colloidal particles) and Brownian Speed.
- When Colloidal particles attract toward Dispersion Medium, they are called Liquid Affinitive Colloids. When the Colloidal particles do not show affinity toward Dispersion Medium, they are called Anti-liquid Colloids. Liquid Affinitive Colloids are more stable and reversible.
- Dialysis (a method of colloidal purification) is used in cleaning the blood with the help of liver machine.

Brownian Movement: The particles of colloidal solution are always in motion, this motion is called Brownian Movement.

Tyndall Effect: when the light is passed through a colloidal solution and the process is observed through a microscope placed vertically to the solution, one observes the colloidal particles glitter like the tip of the pin against dark background. This is called Tyndall Effect.

Types of Colloid: sol, gel, aerosol, froth, pious

- Alum is used for purifying water because it pushes the impurities toward the base of the water.
- **$FeCl_3$** is used in stopping blood leakage because is causes blood clotting.

Carbon and its Compounds

- Allotropy: the matters whose physical properties are different but chemical properties are identical are called 'Allotropes', this event of finding allotropes is called Allotropy.
- Two main types of carbon are diamond and graphite.
- **Hydrocarbon:** the compound of carbon and hydrogen is called hydrocarbon.
- **Hydrocarbon is of three types:** Saturated Hydrocarbon, Unsaturated Hydrocarbon and Aromatic Hydrocarbon.
- **Isomerism:** The relation of two or more compounds composed of the same kinds and numbers of atoms but differ from each other in structural arrangement. These compounds are called the Isomers of each other. It has two main types: Structural and Cis-trans Isomerism.
- **Polymerization:** The molecules of a compound join and make a bigger molecule. The molecules participating in this process are called Monomers and the final product (bigger molecule) is called a Polymer.
- Two examples of natural Polymers are starch and cellulose.
- **Vulcanization:** The process of mixing natural rubber with Sulphur and heating the mixture is called Vulcanization.

Battery

- Battery is the process that converts chemical energy into electrical energy. Batteries are of two types:
- **Primary Battery:** These cannot be recharged and act like galvanized cell. Example: dry cell, mercury cell etc.
- **Secondary Battery:** These can be recharged and act like both galvanized cell and electrical decomposition cell. Example: glass charging battery, Nickel-Cadmium battery.

Sources of Energy

- Renewable sources are available in abundance are they shall never deplete. Example: air, sunlight etc.
- Non-Renewable sources are available in a limited quantity and will go deplete after a certain time. Example: minerals, coal, petroleum, natural gas etc.

Fuel

- Fuel are the matters that generate heat and light when burned.
- When 1 gram of a fuel is burned in the excess exposure to air, then the heat it generates is called the Calorific Value of that fuel.
- The fuel used in the rockets is called propellant. Liquid hydrogen and liquid oxygen are used as chief propellants.

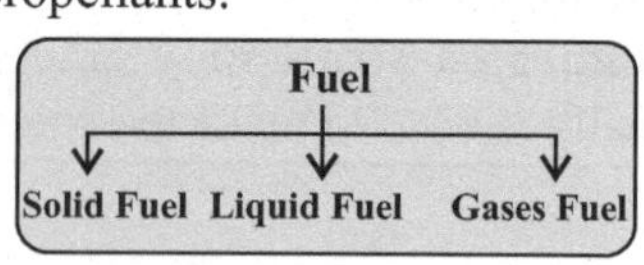

Coal

- Coal is formed by the carbonization of the vegetation. It is found in many forms, e. g. peat coal (60%C), lignite or brown coal (70%C), bituminous coal (80%C) and anthracite coal (90%). Bituminous is the most common type found all around the world.
- **Gaseous Fuel:** natural gas, bio gas, producer

gas, water gas, coal gas etc.

Flame

Flame has three parts:

- **Internal Part:** It appears red because of the presence of the unburnt carbon particles. This part has the lowest temperature.
- **Middle Part:** Looks yellow because of the uncomplete burning of the fuel.
- **Outer Part:** Looks blue because of the complete burning of the fuel. This part has the highest temperature. The goldsmiths use this part of the fire to melt gold.

Fire-extinguisher

Water is a good fire-extinguisher. It turns to vapor after coming in the contact of fire. The vapor surround the burning object and blocks its oxygen supply. Thus, fire is extinguished.

Safety Matchstick

A mixture of Antimony Sulfide and potassium chlorate is applied at one end of the safety matchstick and a mixture of crushed glass and red phosphorous is applied on the matchbox.

Metals

- The elements that loose electrons to become positive (except hydrogen) are called metals. Metals are usually shiny, elastic and malleable.
- **Minerals:** the elements or the compounds of elements that are found inside the earth are called minerals.
- **Ore:** the minerals that can be extracted from metals with simple procedure and are useful.
- **Metallurgy:** The various processes of extracting metals out of ores and their purification is called metallurgy.
- **Gangue:** The impure matter extracted from the ore is called gang.
- **Flux:** The matter that is added into the ore to rid it from gangue is called flux.
- **Slang:** The matter that is formed with the mixture of gangue and flux is called slang.

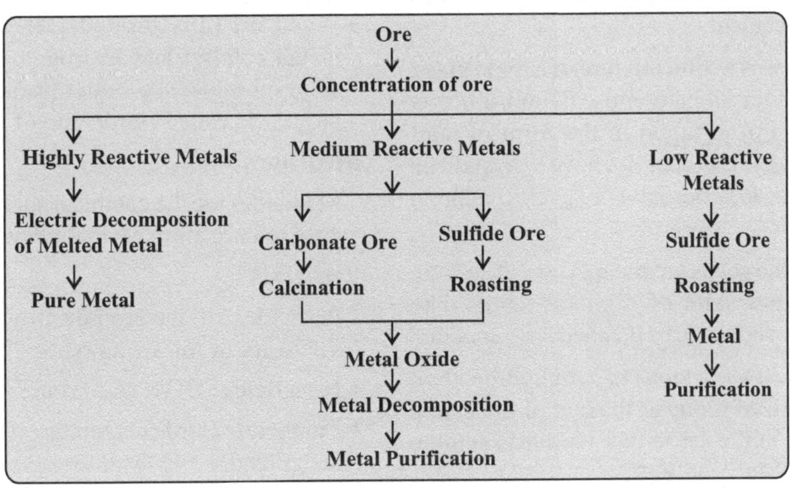

- **Calcination:** in this process the metal ore is heated on the temperature lower than its condensation point to get rid of vaporized impurities.
- **Roasting:** In this process, the metal ore is heated at the temperature lower than its condensation point in the presence of warm air to oxidize the impurities.
- **Smelting:** In this process, the metal is heated at the temperature higher than its condensation point in the presence of coke and flux. This process yields pure metal.

Corrosion

- The wasting of metal surface due to exposure to air and humidity is called Corrosion. It is an electro-chemical process.
- The surface of iron turns brown due to ferric oxide **($Fe_2O_3 \cdot xH_2O$).** This brown surface is called rust.
- Silver turns blackish due to formation of silver sulfide **(Ag_2S)** in the presence of air. Copper's surface turns green due to formation of copper carbonate **$Cu(OH)_2$** . $CuCO_3$.
- Corrosion of iron is called **rusting.**
- Corrosion can be Prevented by electroplating, oil, grease, paint, varnish or galvanization (zinc plating on iron).

Non-metals and Man Made Materials

- Non-metals: modern Periodic Table registers 24 non-metals. 11 of these are gases, 1 is liquid (bromine) and 12 are solid.
- **Cement:** When imestone or chalk is mixed with red sand or rock and the product of this process is cement.
- **Glass:** Glass is a solid mixture of simple glass, silica, sodium silicate and calcium silicate. Glass is a frozen liquid in the form of non-crystal solid. Glass does not have a crystalized form and it does not have a specific melting point.
- **Soap:** All the soaps are the mixture of sodium or potassium salts of high-fat acids. The process of making soaps is called soap-making.
- **Detergent:** It has a long chain of hydrocarbon and a polarized group at the end of the chain. It is better in the sense that its salt is soluble with **Ca^{+2}**, **Mg^{+2}** and **Fe^{+3}**.

Acid and Base

- The matters that turn the blue litmus into red are acids. They usually donate proton into water.
- Base turn the red litmus into blue. Base accept the proton **(H^+)**.

Hard Water

- The water in which bicarbonates of calcium are dissolved is called temporary hard water. In permanent hard water the soluble of calcium and magnesium (I. e. chloride and sulfate) are present.
- Soap does make foam in hard water because of the formation of sulfate chlorite and bicarbonate.
- The temporary hardness of water can be removed by boiling it or adding calcium hydroxide **($Ca(OH)_2$)** into it. This is called Clarke Method.
- To remove the permanent hardness of water, sodium carbonate **(Na_2CO_3)** is added into the water.

Heavy Water

- It is an oxide of heavy hydrogen or deuterium. The molecular weight of heavy water is 20.
- It is used in nuclear reactors.

Hardening of Oil

- When oil (unsaturated fat) is heated with nickel catalyst and hydrogen, it turns into a solid substance, i.e. butter (saturated fat). This process is called Hardening of Oil.

Medicines

Medicines are the chemical substances that are used to cure ailments and alleviation of pain.

Pesticides

Pesticides kill the crop-destroying organisms. There are of following types:

- **Insecticide:** DDT, Gamexane, aluminum
- **Fungicide:** Bordeaux mixture, Organomercury compound
- **Herbicide:** Benzepam, sodium chlorate, sodium arsenate
- **Denticide:** aluminum phosphide
- **Catalysts:** A catalysts is a material that is added to a reaction mixture to accelerate the process but it is itself not participatedis called catalyst and this process is catalysis.

BIOLOGY

Biology is the branch of science concerned with the study of living organisms **(Lamarck and Treviranus, 1802)**. It has three branches: zoology, botany and microbiology. Organisms have been classified into five categories. These categories are: **Monera, Protista, Plantae, Fungi and Animal.** Specie is the basis for this classification.

Some Discoveries Regarding Cells

Scientist	Year	Discovery
Felice Fontana	1781	Nucleoli
Robert Brown	1833	Nucleus
Purkinje	1839	Gave the term Protoplasm
Kolliker	1857	Mitochondria
W. Fleming	1877	Discovered Mitosis
Bender and Bowery	1887	The specie has same number of Chromosomes
Camillo Golgi	1891	Golgi body
C.Benda	1898	Gate the term Mitochondria
W. S. Sutton	1902	Importance of chromosome cell division
Friedrich Meves	1904	Discovery of Plant Mitochondria
J. B. Farmer	1905	Gave the term Amitosis
F. A. Johnson	1909	Formation of Plasma
T. H. Morgan	1933	The role of Chromosomes in Genetics

Cell Science

- The term Protoplasm was given by Purkinje in the year 1839 A. D. this is a thick liquid, colorless, pellucid, ropy and mass containing substance. Protoplasm is responsible for the occurrence of all the biological functions. That is why protoplasm is also called the physical basis of life.
- Two part of protoplasm are Cell Liquid and Nucleus Liquid.
- Two types of Cell: Prokaryotic and Eukaryotic.
- Robert Virchow observed the cell division for the first time in 1855. Cell divisions are mainly of three types: Amitosis, Mitosis and Meiosis.

Genetics

- The transfer of genetic characteristics from generation to generation is called Genetics. Austrian Graham Johann Mendel (1822-1884) first observed Genetics. He is called the Father of Genetics.
- The characteristics of the organism that are observable are called Phenotypes.
- The genetic code of the organism is called Genotype. It is made of genes.

Mendel's Laws

1. Law of Dominance
2. Law of Segregation
3. Law of Independent Assortment

Man Genetics

- W. Walters first gave the name Chromosome in 1888. The genetic substance found in the chromosomes is called Genomes.
- The genes that are found outside the chromosome inside the cell liquid are called Plasma genes.

Organism/ Specie	Chromo somes	Organism/ Specie	Chromo somes
Mosquito	6	House fly	12
Peas	14	Onion	16
Tomato	24	Frog	26
Lemon	18, 36	Cat	38
Mouse	40	Wheat	42
Rabbit	44	Human	46
Potato/Chimpanzee/ Tobacco			48

Difference Between DNA and RNA

DNA	RNA
It has deoxyribose sugar	It has ribose sugar
Its base is adenine, guanine, cytosine and thymine	Uracil takes the place of thymine in the base
This is found mainly in the nucleus	This is found both in the nucleus and cell liquid

Parts of Cell

1. Cell wall 2. Cell membrane 3. Centrosome 4. Endoplasmic reticulum 5 ribosome 6. Mitochondria 7. Golgi body 8. Lysosome 9. Plastid (Chloroplast, Leucoplast and Chromoplast) 10. Vacuoles 11. Nucleus

Organic Evolution

- The evolution of multiple and complex organisms from simple organism is called **Organic Evolution.**
- **Homologous Organ:** The structures which are similar in their morphology, anatomy, genetics and embryology but dissimilar in their function are called **Homologous Organs.**
- **Analogous Organ:** The organs which have the same function but different basic structure are called **Analogous Organs.**
- **Vestigial Organ:** The organs which were fully developed in the ancestors but lost their functional value over time are called **Vestigial Organs.** These organs start to disappear over time.
- **Fossil:** The remains of the organisms which have gone extinct are called **Fossils.** The fossils are found preserved in the rocks near earth's surface. The study of fossils is called **Paleontology.**
- **The branch of biology concerned with the classification of organisms is called Taxonomy.**
- **Carolus Linnaeus** propagated the Binominal **Nomenclature** process of organisms. In this method, the scientific name is made of genus and species of the organism.
- The **modern** process of **nomenclature** is inspired by the process suggested by **Linnaeus.**
- Viruses are miniscule, parasitical, nucleoprotein particles. They get activated inside living organism only. Virus was discovered for the first time in **1892** in tobacco by **Dmitri Ivanovsky.**
- The term Bacteria was given by **Ehrenburg in 1829.**

Botany

- The study of plants and their behavior is called **Botany.**
- **Theophrastus** is considered to be the Father of Botany.
- **Thalophyta is the biggest group of plant world.**
- The study of algae is called **Phycology**.
- **Fungi** is chlorophyll, multinucleate, tissue-less thalophyta. Its cell wall is made of chitin.
- **Bacteria** was discovered by Van **Leeuwen-hoek in 1683.** He is also considered the father of **Bacterial Science.**

Plant Morphology

- The study of appearance and characteristics of different parts of plant like - roots, stems, leaves etc. is called **Morphology.**
- **Roots** are the part of plant that grow downwards, they develop from the radicle. Roots are of two type: **Tap Root and Adventitious Root.**
- The flower contains calyx, corolla, androecium and gynoecium. Androecium is male reproductive organ and gynoecium is female reproductive organ.
- **Androecium** has more than one stamens. **The stamens contain pollen grains.**
- **Gynoecium** has three parts**: ovary, style and stigma.**
- **Pollination:** the process of transfer of pollens from anther to the edge of style is called Pollination. Pollination is of two types: **Self-Pollination and Cross-Pollination.**
- **Fertilization:** is the process of fusion of the female gamete, the ovum or egg, and produced by the pollen grain in the pollen tube. The fertilized egg is called **Zygote.**
- All the fruits have been categorized into three categories: Simple fruits, Aggregate fruits and Composite fruits.
- **Calyx and corolla** take part in the formation of some fruits. These fruits are called **False Fruits.** Example: apple, jack fruit.
- The group of cells with similar origin, structure and functions is called a **Tissue.**

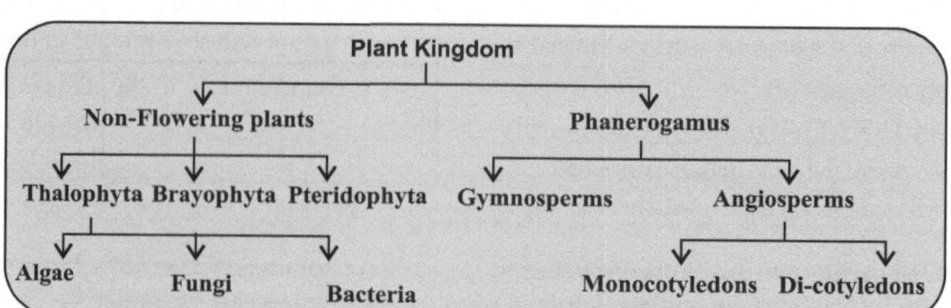

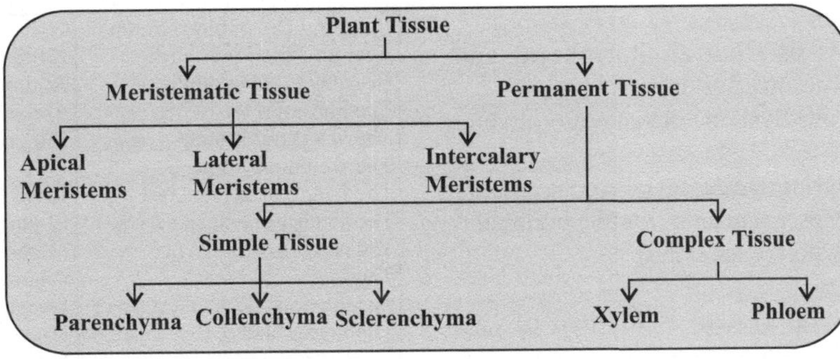

Photosynthesis

- The process by which green plants and some other organisms use sunlight to synthesize nutrients from carbon dioxide and water.

$$6CO_2 + 12H_2O \xrightarrow[\text{Chlorophyll}]{\text{sunlight}} \underset{\text{Glucose}}{C_6H_{12}O_6} + \underset{\text{Water}}{6H_2O} + \underset{\text{Oxygen}}{6O_2}$$

- **Chlorophyll** contains an atom of magnesium in its nucleus.
- Chlorophyll absorbs **violet, blue and red** color from the sunlight.
- Photosynthesis has two stages: **photo chemical and dark chemical.**
- Plant hormones: 1. Auxins 2. Gibberellins 3. Cytokinins 4. Abscisic Acid or ABA 5. Ethylene 6. Florigens 7. Traumatin

Human Anatomy

The functional and structural unit of human body is Cell. Similar cells unite to form Tissues. Tissues unite to form organs and organs unite to form organ-system. Some of the organ-systems in the human body are – digestive system, respiratory circulation, nervous system and endocrine system.

Nutrition

- Carbohydrates, vitamins, protein etc. are nutrients.
- The food that contains all the nutrients in balanced is called **Balanced Diet**.
- 70-80% of human life is made of water.

Respiration

Respiration is an oxidization and energy-providing process. In this process, complex carbonic compounds are broken into simple carbonic compounds.

Blood

- Blood is a thin, acidic (pH 7.4), opaque, slimy liquid made of plasma and blood cells.
- **Plasma:** contains 90-92% water, 1-2% non-carbonic salt, 6-7% plasma protein and 1-2% carbonic compounds.
- **The Red Blood Cells** are oval shaped, bi-convex and nucleic in all the vertebrates except mammals.
- **RBCs** contain respiratory pigment – **Hemoglobin**. It transports the oxygen inside the body.
- **White Blood** Cells are nucleic, pigment-less cells. They protect the body from viruses.
- **Blood Platelets** are colorless and do not have a nucleus. They play an important part in blood clotting.

Circulatory System

- **Open Circulatory** System is found in cockroaches, prone, insects and spider etc.
- **Closed Circulatory** System is found in Annelida, mollusk and all the vertebrates.
- **Heart** is a **big,** muscle constricting, **self-pumping organ.**
- **Fish** have two-chambered, amphibians and reptiles have three-chambered and birds and mammals have four-chambered heart.
- The **normal blood pressure** of an **animal** is **120-80 mmHg.**
- The heartbeat rate of newborn baby is close to **140 beats** per minute.
- Prothrombin, fibrinogen, **Ca^{+2}** and **vitamin K** participate in blood clotting.

Execratory System

- Different animals execrate different types of nitrogen waste.
- The main execratory organ in the human body is **kidney**. This is made of small functional and structural units called **Nephron.**

Nervous System

- This consists of Central, Peripheral and Autonomic Nervous Systems.
- Central Nervous System consists of brain and spinal cord.
- Brain is divided into **three** parts: Prosencephalon (fore-brain), Mesencephalon (middle brain) and Rhombencephalon (back brain).

Skeletal System

Human skeletal system is formed of two parts

1.Axial Skeleton: skull, vertebral column

2.Appendicular Skeleton: girdles, pedal bones

Human Anatomy

Fact	Location/Quantity
Total number of bone	206
The smallest bone	Stapes (in the ear)
The longest bone	Femur (in the thigh)
The number of vertebrae	33
The number of muscles	639
The longest muscle	Sartorius muscle
The length of the large Intestine	1.5 M
The length of the Small Intestine	6.25 M
The weight of the liver (in males)	1.4 – 1.8 KG
The wgt. of the liver (in females)	1.2 – 1.4 KG
The largest gland	Liver
The organ with maximum regeneration capacity	Liver
The organ with minimum regeneration capacity	Brain
The strongest part of the body	Tooth enamel
The longest salivation gland	Parotid gland
The normal temperature of the body	98.4° F (37° C)
The amount of blood in the body	5.5 liter
The average amount of hemo-globin (in males)	13.16g/dl
The average amount of hemo-globin (in females)	11.5-14g/dl
The number of WBCs	5000-10000/cu mm
The smallest WBC	Lymphocyte
The biggest WBC	Monocyte
The life-span of WBCs	120 days
The life-span of RBCs	2-5 days
The time taken in blood clotting	3-6 minutes
Universal Recipient blood group	AB
Universal Donor blood group	O
Average blood pressure	120/80 Hg
Heartbeat rate in adults	72 times per minute
The biggest artery	Abdominal aorta
The weight of kidney	150 gram
The weight of brain	1220-1400 grams
The length of spinal cord	42-45 C.M
The number of cranial nerves	12 pairs
The number of spinal nerves	31 pairs
The longest nerve	Sciatic
The thinnest and smallest nerve	Treaclier
The biggest nerve	Trigeminal
The biggest cell	Nerve cells
The biggest endocrine gland	Thyroid

Some Important Facts Regarding Zoology

Specialty	Name
The biggest mammal	Blue whale
The biggest land-dwelling mammal	Elephant
The biggest bone	Femur
The biggest vein	Inferior vena cava
The biggest land bird	Ostrich
The biggest reptile	Turtle
The most venomous snake in the world	Australian Peninsular Tiger Snake
The smallest sparrow	Hummingbird
Toothless mammal	Ant Eater
The busiest organ of the body	Liver
The heaviest organ of the body	Liver
The heaviest vertebrate	Lumber
The strongest muscle	The jaw muscle
Calories needed in a day (males)	3900 Kilocalories
Calories needed in a day (females)	2400 Kilocalories
The oldest primate	Lemur
The oldest arthropod	Parapets
The oldest mammal	Echidna
The oldest ape	Gibbon
The most venomous Indian snake	King Cobra
Venomous lizard	Heloderma (the Gila Monster)
Venomous fish	Stone fish
Egg-laying mammals	Echidna, Duck Billed Platypus
The smallest mammal	Mole
The fastest flying bird	Peregrine falcon
The fastest running animal	Cheetah
The biggest snake	Python
Nest maker snake	King Cobra

Vitamins: Sources, Functions and Deficiency Effect

Name	Source	Biological Effects	Deficiency Effects
Vitamin – A (Retinol)	Milk, butter, egg, liver and fish oil	Color synthesis, growth and development of epithelium levels	Night-blindness, xerophthalmia, cell-scales, stunted growth, dryness disease, Osteomalacia
Vitamin – D (Calciferol)	Butter, liver, fish oil, lungs, egg, skin and photo - synthesis in yeast	Metabolic of calcium and phosphorus, growth of bones and teeth	Dryness disease, osteomalacia
Vitamin – E (Tocopherol)	Oil, wheat, the yolk of the egg, soybean	Cell protection, growth of birth epithelium, muscle activation	Decline in birth capacity, weakness in reproductive organ and muscles
Vitamin – K (Naphthoquinone)	Green leaves, egg, liver, tomato, cauliflower,soybean, intestinal bacteria	Synthesis of prothrombin in the liver	Deficient blood clotting leading to blood loss
Water Soluble Vitamins			
Vitamin – B_1 (Thymine)	Cereal, legume, soybean, milk, yeast, egg, meat	Necessary metabolic for carbohydrate and amino acid, co-enzyme of enzymes	Beriberi
Vitamin – B_2 (Riboflavin)	Cheese, egg, yeast, green leaves, meat and liver	Element of metabolically important co-enzymes FAD and FMN	Cheilosis
Vitamin – B_3 (Nicotinic Acid)	Yeast, meat, liver, fish, egg, milk, peas, dry fruitsand legume	Element of metabolically important co-enzymes NAD and NAPD	Pellagra
Vitamin – B_5 (Pantothenic Acid)	Egg, liver, meat, milk, tomato, groundnut and sugarcane	Element of catabolism of co-enzyme A	Skin diseases, stunted growth, whitening of hair and decreased reproductive capacity
Vitamin – B_6 (Pyridoxine)	Milk, yeast, cereal, meat, liver and fish	Co-enzyme of the enzymes important in protein metabolism	Blood deficiency, skin diseases and muscle contortion
Vitamin – K	Meat, wheat, egg, fruits groundnut, chocolate, vegetables, and yeast	Co-enzyme in synthesis reactions of many materials	Skin diseases, hair-fall
Folic Acid group	Green leaves, Soyabean, liver, yeast, legume and intestinal bacteria	Growth, formation of blood particles, DNA synthesis	Blood deficiency, stunted growth
Vitamin – B_{12}	Meat, fish, liver, egg, milk, intestinal bacteria	Growth, formation of blood particles, synthesis of nucleic acids	Blood deficiency, nervous system diseases
Vitamin – C	Fruits of the lemon family, tomato, potato vegetables, and other fruits	Inter-cellular cement, formation of collagen, bone matrix and teeth dentine	Scurvy

Medical Instruments

Pacemaker	Heartbeat rate	Electroencephalograph	Brain
Auto-Analyzer	Glucose, cholesterol level detection, urea	Computed Tomography Scan (CT Scan)	Full body
		Electrocardiograph	Heart

Diseases Caused by Bacteria in Humans			
Disease	**Affected Organ**	**Symptoms**	**Bacteria**
Pneumonia	Lungs	Lung infection, pulmonary edema, high fever, difficulty in breathing	Diplococcus pneumoniae
Botulism	Nervous system	Vomiting, double vision	Clostridium botulinum
Leprosy	Skin and nerves	Boils and tumor formation, gradual decaying of hand and feet tissues	Mycobacterium leproae
Tuberculosis	Any part of body especially lungs	Fever, cough, weakness, breathing difficulty, phlegm and blood in saliva	Mycobacterium tuberculosis
Cholera	Intestine	Dehydration, vomiting	Vibrio comma
Diphtheria	Trachea (wind pipe)	High fever, breathing difficulty, choking	Corynebacterium diphtherae
Whooping cough	Respiratory system	Relentless cough, vomiting with cough	Hemophilus pertussis
Plague	Armpits, lungs, RBCs	High fever, swollen lymph glands, fainting	Treponemapestis
Meningitis	Upper membranes of the brain	High fever, fainting, swelling in the brain membranes	Neisseria meningitides
Tetanus	Nerves and muscles	Fainting, lockjaw, jerking of the body	Clostridium tetani
Periodic fever	Intestine	Fever weakness, holes in the intestine during high fever	Salmonella typhi or Eberthella typhosa
Syphilis	Reproductive organ, brain, nervous system	Formation of spots on the reproductive organ, paralysis, grains on the skin, hair-fall pallidum	Treponema

Diseases Caused by Protozoa in Humans			
Disease	Affected Organ	Symptoms	Parasite
Pyorrhea	Teeth-roots and gums	Gum-swelling, blood leakage and pus leakage	Entamoeba gingivalis
Loose-Motion	Large intestine	Swelling and pain in the large intestine, chronic loose-motion	Trichomonas Hominis
Amoebiasis	Large intestine (cologne)	Swelling in the cologne, mucus leakage with loose-motion	Entamoeba histolytica
Dysentery	The initial portions of the intestine	Loose-motion, headache and sometimes causes jaundice	Giardia lamblia
Gonorrhea (in males) and White Discharge (in females)	Urinal tract in males and vagina in females	Burning and pain in urination, discharge of white liquid in women and pain	Trichomonas vaginalis
Loose Motion (Isosporiasis)	Small intestine, blood, bone-marrow, spleen	Contortion in Small Intestine and loose motion	Isospora hominis
Epidemic Encephalitis	Blood, cerebrospinal liquid and central nervous system	High fever, fainting, long sleep	Trypanosoma gambiens
Malaria	Red blood particles, spleen and kidney	High fever, headache, back ache	Plasmodium malariae

Diseases Caused by Fungus

Disease	Affected Organs	Responsible Fungus
Aspergillus Fumigatus	Ears and lungs	Aspergillus Flavus, A. fumigatus
Boils	Throat & mouth	A.Niger and monilia
Cryptococcal disease	Nervous system	Crypotococcus neoformans
Pollen fever	Whole body	Alternaria,and Trichoderma specie
Tetter	Skin	Microsporum lenosun

Diseases Caused by Viruses in Humans

Disease	Affected organs
Tonsil	Parotid saliva glands
Trachoma	Eyes
Dengue	Muscles and joints
Flu or Influenza	Respiratory system
Rabies or hydrophobia	Nervous system
Small-pox	Whole body, especially feet and hands
Jaundice (enters the body via food and water)	Nervous system (destroys the motor nerves of spinal cord)
Herpes	Skin, mucous-membrane
Encephalitis or brain Swelling	Nervous system

Material	Bacteria
Butter Milk	Lactobacillus vulgaricus
Yoghurt	Lactobacillus thermophillus
Curd	Streptococcus lactis
Cheese	Lactobacillus and Streptococcus cremoris
Acetone - Butanol	Clostridium acetobutylicum
Lactic acid	Lactobacillus delbrueckii and Rhizopus oryzae
Lysine	Micrococcus glutamicus
Insulin and interferon	Recombinant and variety of E.coli
Streptokinase	Streptococcus equisimilis
Citric acid	Aspergillus niger
Fumaric acid	Rhizopus nigricans
Gibberellic acid	Furesium Moniliform
Zymes	Saccharomyces species
Pectinus	Aspergillus venti
Beer, rum, scotch, alcohol	Saccharomyces species

Diseases and the Organs Affected by Them

Disease	Affected Organs
Arthritis	Joint swelling
Diphtheria	Throat, wind pipe
Echzema	Skin
Jaundice	Kidney
Pleurisy	Chest
Pyorrhea	Teeth and gums
Rheumatism	Joints
Tetanus	Nervous system, muscles
Leprosy	Skin, nerves
Cholera	Intestine, food canal
Whooping cough	Respiratory system
Cataract, glaucoma	Eyes
Tetter	Skin
Cryptococcal disease	Nervous system
Hepatitis - B	Liver
Trachoma	Kidney, eyes and pancreatitis
Diabetes	Pancreatitis, kidney and eyes
Goiter	Thyroid gland
Parkinson	Brain
Pneumonia	Lungs
Typhoid	Intestine
Rickets	Bones
Syphilis	Reproductive organ
Loose-motion	Large intestine
Diarrhea	Starting point of the intestine
Gonorrhea and White Discharge	Urinary tract
Isosporiasis	Blood, bones and spleen
Athlete foot	Feet
Boils	Throat and mouth
Meningitis	Spinal cord and brain

Important Antibiotics, their Source and Functions

Antibiotic	Name of the Microbe	Function
Penicillin	Penicillium notatum	Tonsillitis, prevention from rheumatism fever
Griseofulivin	Penicillium griseofulivin	Prevention from tetter
Streptomycin	Streptomycin griseofulivin	Prevention from T.B, meningitis, pneumonia
Chloramphenicol	Streptomyces venezuelei	Prevention from typhoid and intestinal infection
Tetracycline	Streptomyces aureofaciens	Prevention from viral, pneumonia, whooping cough and eye infection
Terramycin	Streptomyces rimosus	Prevention from viral, typhoid and intestinal infection
Erythromycin	Streptomyces erithrius	Prevention from whooping cough and diphtheria
Bacitracin	Bacillus licheniformus	Prevention from reticulitis lymphonima

Medicinal Plants

Normal Name	Botanical Name	Family	Main Part of the Plant
Sarpgandha	Rauvolfia Serpentina	Apocynaceae	Roots
Opium poppy	Papaver Somniferum	Papaveraceae	Capsule fruit
Belladonna	Atropa Belladonna	Solanaceae	Dry leaves and roots
Datura	Datura Stramonium	Solanaceae	Fruits and juice
Amla	Emblica Officinalis	Euphorbiaceae	Fruits
Strychnine	Strychnon nux-vomica	Loganiaceae	Seeds

Important Facts about Botany

Specialty	Name
The smallest virus	Parvovirus (18-26 nm)
The biggest virus	TMV (300 nm)
Parasite	Pox (280 nm)
The smallest bacteria	Dialister (2 m)
The biggest bacteria	Beggiatoa Mirabilis
The smallest bryophyte	Jupcis
The biggest bryophyte	Dawsonia
The biggest pteridophyte	Cyathea
The smallest gymnosperm	Zamia Pygmaea
The biggest gymnosperm	Sequoia Gigantea
The smallest angiosperm	Wolffia
The biggest angiosperm	Eucalyptus Regnans
The smallest flower	Rafflesia Arnoldii
The biggest flower	Orchid
The broadest leaf	Victoria Regia
The heaviest wood	Guaiacum Officinale
The biggest unicellular plant	Acetabularia
The amphibians of the plant world	Bryophyte
Vascular Cryptogams	Pteridophyte
Walking fern	Adiantum
Maidenhair fern	Adiantum
Maidenhair tree	Ginkgo Biloba
Most protein-rich algae	Spirulina

Fruits and their Edible Parts

Fruit	Part
Papaya	Middle membrane
Coconut	Embryo sac
Tomato	Ovule and fruit membrane
Apple	Torus
Pear	Torus
Mango	Middle membrane
Banana	Middle and internal membrane
Guava	Ovule and fruit membrane
Grape	Ovule and fruit membrane
Orange	juicy fibers
Jack fruit	Perianth and seeds
Groundnut	Cotyledon and embryo
Wheat	Embryo sac and embryo
Cashew	Cotyledon and pedicel
Grams	Cotyledon and embryo
Litchi	Aril
Mulberry	Juicy perianth
Pineapple	Perianth/perigone

- Oxygen was not present at the planet when life first appeared here.
- Bones are strong as concrete and solid like granite.
- Almost 150 lakh cells get destroyed in the body every second.
- Kidney weighs almost 140 grams.
- Human body has almost 50 lakh hairs.